Praise for *Why Don't They Just Get a Job?*

This richly detailed, informative book shares the hard-learned experience of Cincinnati Works in helping thousands of hard-to-employ men and women find good jobs and not only stay in them, but advance in them to achieve meaningful and productive lives. It demonstrates how a focus on achieving measurable outcomes based on continued learning and experimentation and a deep empathy for each person can produce results most would consider unachievable. Well worth reading for anyone confronting one of the major issues our nation is facing, i.e., helping individuals find a meaningful, rewarding, and productive career.

–John E. Pepper, retired chairman and CEO,
The Procter & Gamble Company

Cincinnati Works' staff looks at each person and asks, "What does this person need to be successfully employed?" The differentiator at Cincinnati Works is that the poor are treated with empathy—not like second-class citizens. It is a spiritual organization. You have to believe in a higher power to do this work. Dave and Liane introduced metrics from the beginning, which is almost unheard of with nonprofits, and have engaged in vigorous experimentation. What they've done is brilliant.

–Clay Mathile, chairman of Aileron, an entrepreneurial
training center, and former owner and chairman of
The Iams Company

Breaking the chains of poverty requires hard work, patience, tremendous focus, and faith—both on the side of the poor and those offering a hand up. Cincinnati Works offers a triumphant new model for helping the poor move to economic sustainability. This nonprofit, which gives people the tools to develop good habits and make good decisions, deserves to be widely imitated in communities across the nation. It's a win-win for the poor and the businesses that hire them.

> –Sean Covey, senior vice president of innovations and products at FranklinCovey, and author of the international bestseller *The 7 Habits of Highly Effective Teens* and *The 6 Most Important Decisions You'll Ever Make: A Guide for Teens*

Cincinnati Works continues to impress our foundation with its available statistics showing growing numbers of clients benefiting from its programs and services. This demonstrates that Cincinnati Works' mission statement works, and people are able to maintain employment with a strategy that makes the difference.

> –Dixie Barker, executive director of the Federated Department Stores Foundation

Cincinnati Works provides a win-win model for businesses and the people they help to become self-sufficient. This innovative nonprofit has tackled its very ambitious vision of eliminating poverty by helping one person at a time—and has some striking results to show for it. A must-read for anyone interested in businesses doing well by doing good.

> –Elizabeth Cogswell Baskin, author of *How to Run Your Business Like a Girl,* and CEO of Tribe, Inc.

A lot of programs claim to address the basic issue of helping people get jobs, but Cincinnati Works uniquely fills that role and provides documented, measurable results.

> –James Schwab, Cincinnati market president, U.S. Bank

The Cincinnati Works program provides the opportunity for a community to work to break the cycle of poverty. It has measurable results, does what it says it will do, and acts as a prudent steward of the assets it has received. Cincinnati Works works.

–Thomas G. Cody, vice chairman, Macy's

Finding a job is important ... retaining a job is necessary to building a life. Cincinnati Works has given "life" and opportunity to so many who had no hope for a future. This book can be a guide for all who read it.

–Carl H. Lindner, Jr., chairman of the board, American Financial Corporation

An inspiring read. No other program or approach so purposefully balances the integrity of every human being with personal accountability and meaningful work. Kudos to the founders of Cincinnati Works, its members, employer-partners, supporters, and the city of Cincinnati itself.

–Richard T. Farmer, chairman of the board, Cintas Corporation

What Cincinnati Works understands is the heartache, hopelessness, and lack of trust the chronically unemployed deal with every day. Dave and Liane have blended basic job skills, support systems, and faith—which starts the launch of hope and confidence. You will see how the suppressed spirit grows, allowing the escape from a lifetime of depression to a bright future. The successes are incredible.
–David Herche, chairman and CEO, Enerfab, Inc.

Cincinnati Works is an employment initiative with great vision, focused strategy, and strong results provided in a culture of caring. United Way is proud to be an original and continuing funding partner. Cincinnati Works deserves to be a model for

any organization looking for programs that work, and this book deserves to be read by anyone who wants to help people get back to work.

—Robert C. Reifsnyder, president and CEO, United Way of Greater Cincinnati

Dave gave up a lucrative accounting practice to devote the rest of his life, alongside his wife, Liane, to helping others. Their approach is to instill hope that things will get better in those who are down and out. They infuse the confidence in those same people that they can hold down a job and, finally, place them in jobs in which they can and will succeed. This truly is an altruistic and humanitarian success story of the highest order!

—Robert H. Castellini, chairman, Castellini Company, and president and CEO, Cincinnati Reds

Liane and Dave Phillips took an idea, formed a concept, built a model, polished the model, and now you have Cincinnati Works. Liane, in partnership with her indefatigable husband Dave, took an idea and unleashed an unbelievably powerful force. Faced with retirement and the sense that it was time to return home, Liane and Dave decided to dedicate the rest of their lives to improving the lives of others in their beloved Cincinnati. Working for a dollar a year and toiling for some 15 years, they made Cincinnati Works evolve from a concept to a working, doable business that enables the disadvantaged of all ages to receive intensive but short-duration training and counseling and convert this experience into meaningful work—a remarkable feat that has been attempted before but never perfected like it has been at Cincinnati Works. Cincinnatians are extremely fortunate that Dave and Liane call Cincinnati home.

—John F. Barrett, chairman, president, and CEO, Western & Southern Financial Group

WHY DON'T THEY JUST GET A JOB?

*One couple's mission to end
poverty in their community*

Liane Phillips and
Echo Montgomery Garrett

Why Don't They Just Get a Job? One couple's mission to end poverty in their community. Revised edition.
Liane Phillips and Echo Montgomery Garrett
277 pp.

© 2010 Liane Phillips. Revised 2016.
Published by aha! Process, Inc.

aha! Process, Inc.
P.O. Box 727
Highlands, TX 77562-0727
(800) 424-9484 ■ (281) 426-5300
Fax: (281) 426-5600
Website: www.ahaprocess.com

Library of Congress Control Number: 2009913990

ISBN 13: 978-938248-81-8

Copy editing by Jesse Conrad
Book design by Paula Nicolella
Cover design by Naylor Design

Printed in the United States of America

"Give a man a fish, and you feed him for a day. Teach a man to fish, and he feeds himself for a lifetime."

—Adapted by Dave Phillips from Lao Tzu

This book is dedicated to all the members of Cincinnati Works. Their tenacity in overcoming barriers and moving toward self-sufficiency continues to amaze me. We celebrate the victories of the determined people who have succeeded in overcoming poverty and honor and encourage those who are still striving for economic freedom and dignity.

CONTENTS

Acknowledgments

Without our partners, funders, volunteers, employers, and other community organizations, there would be no Cincinnati Works story.

Many thanks to the Cincinnati Works staff, who gave of their time to read the manuscript and provide suggestions that were most helpful. Special thanks goes to Glenna Parks, director of operations; to Beth Smith, former president of Cincinnati Works; and to Dave, my partner at home and in the office. Their contributions were invaluable.

FOREWORD

When working with people in poverty, one of the most common refrains is: *"Why don't they just get a job?"* To individuals with a good work history, the answer to this question is a no-brainer. Stories about work are passed intergenerationally: how to relate to supervisors, the rules of work (get there on time, stay busy, etc.), what happens when you work for yourself, how to balance work and a personal life, and so forth. But one of the characteristics of generational poverty is the instability of work. One of the most common phrases you hear in a neighborhood of generational poverty is: "I was looking for a job when I found this one." The concept of a career is largely nonexistent, and if you don't like your boss, you quit—on the spot.

Liane and Dave Phillips have provided a self-supporting model for development of human capacity in the workplace. Theirs is a story about faith—faith that people in poverty are able and are problem solvers, faith in the business sector that has used a business mindset to eliminate workplace barriers for people in poverty, and faith that Cincinnati Works treats its employees fairly and provides an employee assistance program—tailored to the needs of the working poor—that's second to none.

I first met Dave and Liane in Cincinnati several years ago. They had read my books, *A Framework for Understanding Poverty* and *Bridges Out of Poverty,* and had used them as resources to understand and provide the supports needed for individuals from poverty to get and maintain employment. They showed me their facility, and I met several of their staff members. I was very impressed by the staff, the philosophy, and the results they were getting—and I was struck by the warm, friendly feel of a healthy working environment.

The things that make Cincinnati Works stand out include the following:

- No government funding
- High number of clients who are employed, particularly among poor and minority males
- The ability of the team to identify barriers to steady attendance at work, along with the creative and rapid ways in which those barriers are overcome
- Successful interventions for former gang members who wish to become employed
- The businesslike, no-nonsense manner in which the nonprofit is run
- The way in which every individual is valued for his or her unique abilities, yet is seen as part of the team (after all, those who seek work though Cincinnati Works become lifelong members of this special organization)

Indeed, one-on-one human support is a hallmark of Cincinnati Works. For example, the Cincinnati Works leadership folks discovered that more than 60% of the clients suffered from depression. So a local hospital foundation agreed to supply an onsite, full-time mental health specialist who meets with the clients. Cincinnati Works teaches the clients the "hidden rules" of the workplace, how to handle a difficult boss, and never to quit a job until they call and talk to someone at the Cincinnati Works office. They have identified both the barriers and the supports necessary for employment and financial success. While money gets one beyond survival mode, it doesn't change thinking, nor does it automatically develop human capacity. Cincinnati Works successfully addresses these systemic and underlying issues.

Dave Phillips retired from his career with accounting firm Arthur Andersen to join Liane in starting Cincinnati Works, which has been phenomenally successful in its short history of just more than a decade. My company, aha! Process, Inc., recommends it as a model to other communities.

Many believe that the first major revolution in the world was the development of agriculture, whereby people could become stable and begin asset development, and that the second major revolution was the development of industry, in which tools and machines were used to do much of the work. But for the next century (or longer), it will be community and national sustainability that will carry us forward: the ability to develop our human capacity, our intellect, and our resources, yet maintain them for the next generation. Dave and Liane have provided us a model to enable all individuals, regardless of their resource base, to contribute to the larger society and provide meaning, pride, and support for themselves and others. There are three principal factors that move one out of poverty: employment, relationships with people different from you (bridging social capital), and education. Cincinnati Works addresses all three. Most importantly, this organization is a replicable model to develop sustainable communities that can address a serious social need—employment in generational poverty. Bottom line: Cincinnati Works works.

–Ruby K. Payne, Ph.D.
President, aha! Process, Inc.

INTRODUCTION

*"Hope begins in the dark, the stubborn hope
that if you just show up and try to do the
right thing, the dawn will come. You wait
and watch and work: You don't give up."*

–Anne Lamott

"Are they Christians or just insane?" our son's friend asked when he heard of our plans to start Cincinnati Works with the lofty mission of ending poverty in our community.

"Both," Scott replied.

In retrospect, our son was right, although we prefer to substitute the word *naïve* for *insane.*

As my husband Dave contemplated his retirement in 1994 after a 32-year career with accounting firm Arthur Andersen, I encouraged him to come up with a plan well in advance. I had retired from teaching remedial reading in the public school system eight years prior and filled my days volunteering, primarily for children's causes.

For the past five years Dave had routinely worked 100-hour weeks in the high-octane job that he loved. In just seven years he'd racked up more than five million frequent flyer miles.

I anticipated that a sudden cessation of activity would be disastrous for both of us—though spending the month of February in Hawaii was mutually appealing. We wrestled with what was most important at this time in our lives. Was it more money in the bank? Was it quality of life?

Escaping to a second home during Ohio's cold months did not sound attractive to either one of us. As much as we relish the grand adventure of travel, living out of a suitcase grows stale. And although we lived in a country club subdivision, we didn't even play golf.

Both born in Ohio at the tail end of the Great Depression, Dave and I grew up in blue collar families of German descent and limited financial means. We were college sweethearts. After our marriage and the completion of Dave's military service, we settled in Cincinnati and raised three sons. With the exception of two business transfers that took Dave to the West Coast, Cincinnati has always been our home. As Dave approached retirement, we had many long discussions and prayed together about what our next chapter might look like. Because we had received so much from the community where we raised our family, we came to believe that it was God's will for us to devote our retirement years to giving back to that community.

Then, at age 56, Dave faced the biggest decision of his career. Arthur Andersen—where he had started in September 1962, straight out of college, making $535 a month—offered him a plum position. The new position would be the capstone of a great career, and taking it on would allow him to finish his career with a flourish by the firm's mandatory retirement age of 62. There was one catch: The position required a move out of the country.

I comforted myself with Dave's promise that, once he retired, we would tackle our dream of working together for a cause we had yet to agree on. But that day now seemed an eternity away.

One Sunday morning that spring of 1994, after church service at College Hill Presbyterian, Dave said, "Liane, I heard a message from God. It happened during the service. I'm going to take early retirement. I don't know exactly what God wants from us, but I know it has something to do with serving the poor."

"Dave, are you sure?" I asked, thunderstruck. From our many conversations it seemed that he had been leaning heavily toward taking the new role he'd been offered at work.

"I'd always wondered what people meant when they said they'd received a calling," Dave said. "I've never been more certain of anything in my life. I have been trying to bargain with God because I wanted to take the new job. You know the money never was that important to me, but I rationalized that we could do so much more good if we had it. The truth is that I wanted that one last challenge. Wrestling with Him over this thing is what's been keeping me up at night."

Tears blurred my vision. The man who had captured my heart when we were 19 years old now filled it with excitement and anticipation.

"You cannot imagine how happy I am at this moment," I said. "I believe it is God's will for us to devote our retirement years to giving back. I just never expected to get an early start. Whatever we end up doing, I know it will be an adventure."

Dave said, "I don't understand the timing, but God wants me to start this new chapter with you right now."

Over lunch we bowed our heads in prayer. Dave's prayer was a simple one: "God, do with this dream what you will—we're just along for the ride."

Although the message Dave got was clear that we were supposed to do something to help disadvantaged people, we didn't have a clue about what "doing something" might look like. We spent the next six months talking to folks and mulling over various possibilities.

Then our daughter-in-law Jenny sent us an article from Cleveland's *The Plain Dealer* about an organization called Cleveland Works. The nonprofit welfare-to-work agency had been operating for about a decade and moved families off the welfare rolls by placing adults in jobs and helping them keep those jobs. This kind of assistance particularly appealed to the accountant in Dave. We scheduled a visit.

Housed in a nondescript building in downtown Cleveland, Cleveland Works' lobby overflowed, mostly with African-American women. (We later learned that the vast majority of Cleveland Works' clients were single, African-American mothers.) The congenial staff helped people fill out job applications, figure out childcare issues, navigate transportation challenges, and deal with other problems that made getting and keeping a job a daunting task.

Cleveland Works offered various types of skills training to bring the clients up to speed for the entry-level positions they were seeking. It also acted as a go-between for employers and the entry-level, newly hired Cleveland Works clients. The friendly and professional counselors we met emphasized the importance of job retention.

After spending a day with the Cleveland Works staff and the people the agency served, Dave and I walked back to our car. Features of the program that stood out to us were that it took a holistic approach to the job seeker, the environment had the feel of an employment agency, barriers were removed by the support services offered, a counselor assisted the job seeker with job retention at the place of employment, and it supplied employers with qualified, entry-level workers.

"I know what you're thinking," I said.

"Yep," Dave said. "We just found our 'what.'"

After Dave and I agreed that we would launch a jobs program that would help the poor and chronically underemployed in Greater Cincinnati, we spent the next month visiting other successful models around the country. Washington Works, in Seattle, concentrated on moving female recipients of Aid to Families with Dependent Children into jobs. Hope, a program in Milwaukee, focused on job seekers formerly on welfare and those with more serious problems. The agency gave them a stipend while they were being trained for private-sector employment.

Orange County Works, in California, was designed to help foster children who typically leave the system when they "age out" at 18 and yet often have few connections or skills to help them obtain jobs. Emancipated foster youth are at high risk of homelessness, incarceration, prostitution, and drug addiction.

The most effective model we saw was Job Net in Portland, Oregon. Managed by the Portland Development Commission, the agency concentrated on job acquisition and retention and was the sole-source provider of entry-level employees for more than 200 Portland corporations. Job Net reduced the number of people living in poverty in Portland by at least 3% per year in three out of four years.

After our whirlwind fact-finding mission, we returned to Cincinnati all but certain that we were on the right path. I was eager to get started right away on a jobs program of our own design. But Dave, who had spent his career as an auditor and exercised caution in every situation, insisted we get answers to three main questions before proceeding: Are there a significant number of poor people in the Greater Cincinnati region who need help making the transition out of poverty? Are there decent jobs available for them? And is there a need for another jobs program in our community to connect people with available jobs?

"We cannot ask anybody for money until we're absolutely certain this idea is viable and needed," said Dave. We invested money from our retirement fund to do the necessary research and determine if we were on the right track.

To answer the first question we hired Applied Information Resources, a nonprofit public policy research organization, to focus on the degree of poverty in our region and determine who was affected by poverty and in what numbers. The 1990 U.S. Census counted more than 186,000 adults and 175,000 children living in poverty in Greater Cincinnati, which also encompasses northern Kentucky. Dave and I were shocked to learn that in the 10 years since the 1980 census, Cincinnati's poverty rate had skyrocketed from 12% to 24%. Two groups suffered the most: African Americans and Appalachians each made up 40% of those in poverty. Bottom line: Plenty of folks were in dire straits and needed help.

Mercer Management Consulting Firm of Lexington, Massachusetts, addressed the second question for us. The firm surveyed a sample of full-time jobs paying $6–9 an hour that also provided healthcare benefits. The research showed that

200 businesses had an immediate need for more than 1,200 unskilled, entry-level employees. When those results were projected over our entire region, the firm estimated at least 10,000 jobs were unfilled due to a lack of qualified applicants. We were taken aback by the abundance of jobs available. Now we knew that many unskilled, entry-level jobs that provided a decent wage and healthcare benefits were going unfilled in our region.

Professor Steven R. Howe of the University of Cincinnati researched the answer to our third and final question. He conducted an extensive survey of job development and job placement organizations. His research revealed that the Ohio Bureau of Employment had placed 3,000 people in the previous year. Twenty other organizations combined to place a total of 4,222 people. Data were not available to show how many of those jobs were full-time, how much they paid, or whether they offered health benefits. No data were available on how many of those people kept their jobs for a full year.

When we compared the number of people living in poverty to the number of recorded jobs obtained in the previous year, we understood that all the answers to our questions pointed to an undeniable need for the type of organization we dreamed of building.

Cincinnati Works was born.

When people found out what we were attempting to do, we were asked over and over again a question that grated on our nerves: "Why don't they just get a job?"

That's the million-dollar question when it comes to the chronically unemployed. (A million dollars also happens to be the minimum cost to society over the lifespan of each and every household in poverty in the United States.) We have fought to find the answers to that loaded question, born of the frustration and lack of understanding many middle class and wealthy people demonstrate for the poor. We committed ourselves to learning what individuals in poverty need instead of trying to impose our ideas about what would work. A vital part of our mission became educating our community and ourselves about the many obstacles the poor face in their journey to self-sufficiency.

While our program may sound simple and familiar, the approach that we developed over time is drastically different from most. Rather than simply focusing on helping the unemployed get a job like traditional job services do, we focus on job retention and advancement. For our fully loaded cost of about $2,500 per person, we provide every job seeker who successfully completes our free, mandatory, one-week job readiness workshop with a lifetime of free, ongoing staff support during job searches and to help members retain their jobs.

This minimal investment in a person struggling in poverty boggles my mind when I compare it with the $30,000 per year one household in our region living in poverty costs society, according to the University of Cincinnati.

For members who need extra assistance—for example, more computer skills or a driver's license—to advance on the job, Cincinnati Works invests an additional average of $600 per person annually. We treat each person in poverty as an individual who deserves dignity and kindness. We help systematically tackle each person's barriers to solid employment. Our strong partnership with employers anchors our win-win approach. We give the poor a hand up—not a handout—and all the support they need on their journey out of poverty.

The fruit of our labor of love is a radical new model in the multi-billion-dollar-a-year workforce development industry. We have used this model to help more than 8,000 men and women since we opened our doors in 1996. One of the most impressive statistics shows that Cincinnati Works members achieve a stellar 70+% job retention rate after a year. A lack of job stability often pockmarks the job histories of the poor, making it difficult for them to improve their circumstances.

When you consider that many of our members have been receiving government assistance for years, and that many come from generational poverty, the number of our members who retain jobs becomes even more impressive. The majority of job programs—most of which are open only to women with dependent children, as stipulated by the government in return for federal funding—don't track job retention. Those that do generally report an abysmal 15–20% job retention rate after a year.

In our region today, nearly 25% of the population isn't economically self-sufficient. That's more than 400,000 people—nearly half of them children—who subsist on less than $19,600 a year for a family of four. In the last three years alone, 1,900 Cincinnati Works members—about two-thirds of whom are parents with children age 18 or younger at home—have earned more than $35 million in wages at an average wage of $9.03 an hour. A critical factor in their ability to get out of poverty is that these jobs come with health insurance benefits for their families.

For every 1,000 people who move out of poverty and become economically self-sufficient, society saves more than $30 million in annual support services. Consider the enormous cost benefit to businesses that now have more stable entry-level workers available to them. Factor in the reduction in societal ills disproportionately represented among the poor like crime, incarceration, school dropouts, domestic violence, child abuse and neglect, and poor physical and mental health, and Cincinnati Works' investment of about $2,500 per person in poverty yields an immense payoff.

Many of us dream of making a difference. Many of us say that with time and money on our hands we would help the poor. But our culture demands and values quick fixes to any and every problem. Many view figuring out ways to help people who are living below the poverty line as too daunting a task, almost a quixotic pursuit.

Now recognized as one of the nation's leading poverty-to-work programs and one of the few nonprofits ever highlighted in the *Harvard Business Review*, Cincinnati Works has long since outstripped our original vision. When we started out, we thought we'd be doing well if we helped 2,000 people find jobs in our lifetime—a number we've long since surpassed. We've even launched a pilot program to help teens and young adults who have aged out of foster care find and retain jobs.

In 2007 we were asked to provide the work component for the Cincinnati Initiative to Reduce Violence, a groundbreaking cooperative effort among law enforcement, government, and several other agencies to help some of the most violent gang members, drug dealers, and felons in our city establish law-abiding lives. Since then our staff has evaluated more than 400 former gang members. Some were referred to other agencies for help with problems ranging from addiction to serious mental health concerns. But more than 275 have successfully completed our job readiness workshop and found jobs at last count. When we started, officials who had worked with a similar project in Boston that didn't have a work component predicted that we would be lucky to place three or four former gang members in jobs each year. We were glad to be able to far exceed their expectations.

We share these stories in the hope that they will inspire others to think outside the box and find new solutions to tough problems. You can make a difference. *Don't listen to anyone who tells you a problem is too big to tackle.* Being stubborn Midwesterners, Dave and I ignored the naysayers—those who wondered out loud what two retired, upper middle class suburbanites could possibly know about making a meaningful difference for the poor—and those who were too polite to do more than whisper their doubts to each other when they thought we couldn't hear.

In these pages I share the triumphs, joy, and heartbreaks that our members, our staff, Dave, and I have experienced along this journey. You'll meet the man who has never held a steady job and who is so ashamed he can't hold your gaze, the single mom with three children who has been in hiding from domestic violence and who hasn't had a job in a decade, and the high school dropout who reads on a second-grade level and struggles to fill out a job application.

These are the faces of Cincinnati Works' members, people society has written off as beyond hope. Yet with the support and caring of the Cincinnati Works staff, thousands have tenaciously risen to the challenge and demonstrated that they are fully capable of achieving stable employment with decent wages and health benefits. They have taken the necessary steps to break the chains of poverty.

There are no composite characters in this book. In cases when someone asked not to be identified, we've used a pseud-onym. Some people are briefly mentioned, while others' stories are woven throughout the book. Many of our members have become part of our extended family, and five have joined our small, close-knit staff. However, not all of our members' stories have happy endings. These are real people facing incredible odds as they struggle to get on firm financial footing.

The majority of our members are African American, which reflects the population near our main location in downtown Cincinnati. But poverty knows no racial boundaries. The people we serve come from a variety of ethnic backgrounds. In fact, we keep a map in the office with pins that show all the places around the world our members are from.

Dave and I understand all too well that there is no "one size fits all" solution for the multifaceted quandaries facing today's leaders in regard to poverty. As I write these words, *more than one out of every 10 people* (12.6% of the population) in the United States lives below the poverty line. That's 37 million people each living on less than $9,800 a year. In 2005 the poverty rate for children under 18 hovered at a shocking 17.6% and continues to grow. *Another 27 million Americans live precariously close to that line* and well below what it takes to be economically self-sufficient. Poverty is a community problem. Eliminating it takes a community solution. However, many of the barriers to employment faced by the poor are the same throughout the nation, and the challenges of serving them are universal. By heeding the lessons we've learned, those who desire to aid people in poverty will find a successful formula that can be readily tailored to the needs of the impoverished in their own communities.

Imagine the immeasurable but powerful ripple effect of thousands of individuals thriving in the work world, able to make their own way and take care of their families without outside assistance. Now think about replicating our documented results in communities all over the nation. This process is slow, hard work, but the payoff strictly in dollars and cents is immense; in terms of restoring human dignity, stabilizing families, and tapping into human potential, it is priceless.

Our fervent hope is that others will adopt the concepts embodied by Cincinnati Works and that our model will take root, grow, and thrive throughout our nation. This model allows impoverished families to experience the dignity that comes with self-sufficiency and, most importantly, brings hope for the future to the millions of men, women, and children who reside in the long shadow of poverty.

–Liane Phillips

CHAPTER 1

Startup: An Audacious Vision
Summer 1994

"There will always be poor people in the land.
Therefore I command you to be openhanded
toward your brothers and toward the poor
and needy in your land."
—Deuteronomy 15:11

When Dave turned down the position, opted for early retirement at age 56, and told the partners at Arthur Andersen what he planned to do for the remainder of his life, they were dumbfounded.

"I think they expected to haul me out kicking and screaming at the mandatory retirement age of 62," he told me when he related their reaction to his announcement. His colleagues at Arthur Andersen couldn't reconcile the hard-charging, no-nonsense Dave they knew with the one who insisted he would be content sharing a tiny office with his wife and working with the poor.

Some of our closest friends thought we had gone a little crazy. Even our own sons were skeptical. Word got back to Dave that our oldest son Scott told friends he was betting our foray into the nonprofit world wouldn't last a year.

When Dave first started talking to the business community about our plans, more than a few asked, "What do you know about poor people?"

"I don't know much," Dave admitted. "But Liane and I are bound and determined to devote the rest of our lives to figuring out what we can."

We didn't pretend to have all the answers. What we did have was a big dose of optimism and a commitment to challenge the myths about people in poverty. Dave and I vowed to do our best to see the world through their eyes. There had to be a better way to connect the poor who were able and willing to work with the thousands of entry-level jobs that were going unfilled in Greater Cincinnati.

About the same time that we decided to start Cincinnati Works, Dave was approached by a newly formed nonprofit group called Downtown Cincinnati, Inc. (DCI) that was dedicated to the growth and revitalization of downtown. DCI's search committee asked Dave to lead the new nonprofit as its chief executive officer.

Dave explained that we were committed to starting a jobs program and asked if it could be included as a part of DCI. The business leaders recognized that breathing new life into downtown and attracting new businesses and investment to the area meant paying equal attention to the people side of the equation. They enthusiastically agreed to Dave's request.

Like many inner cities, downtown Cincinnati had slipped economically. The go-go economy of the 1990s had failed to touch its streets, which had an oversupply of unoccupied commercial space and few attractions or restaurants that could serve as a draw to the area. Many of the jobs—especially for entry-level workers—had migrated to the suburbs.

Yet 95% of the poor who so desperately needed these jobs and who lived in the inner city did not have access to a reliable vehicle. The bus lines were their only source of transportation and often didn't serve the areas where the better paying jobs were found. Many of the working poor were single moms with an average of 2–3 kids. They typically got up and spent hours a day on a bus, dropping off kids at school or day care, and then went to low-wage jobs with no benefits.

Dave's charge was to strategize and help make downtown once again thrive as an exciting place to play, work, and live. It was a tall order, but Dave agreed to head up DCI as a dollar-a-year volunteer. In exchange, Cincinnati Works could use the infrastructure of DCI and operate under its nonprofit Internal Revenue Service status as a 501(c)(3). It was a win-win proposition that allowed us to minimize our startup costs. After decades of marriage, Cincinnati Works afforded us the opportunity to work side by side at something we were both passionate about.

"Good thing I never learned to like golf," Dave teased.

The morning of September 1, 1994 marked the first day of Dave's official retirement and the start of our new life. I was still in the process of recovering from a recent surgery, and I awoke in terrible pain.

"Why don't you just stay here?" Dave asked. "I can handle the interview with the reporter. You don't have to go."

"No, no, I'll be fine," I insisted.

Of course, I didn't want to miss our first official day together, but what Dave didn't know was that 120 of our friends, colleagues, and business associates awaited us downtown at the Banker's Club. He had already had retirement parties in Chicago and Los Angeles, but we hadn't done anything in our hometown. People had flown in from Los Angeles, Indianapolis, and Chicago for the celebration.

Before heading for the party, we attended a prayer service at a Presbyterian church downtown. During the service the minister asked God to be with us and guide us. Then we made our way to the Banker's Club, perched on the 30th floor of an office building overlooking downtown Cincinnati, where Dave thought we were having a breakfast meeting with a reporter who wanted to interview us about our new venture.

Instead, when we came through the doors we were greeted by a whole roomful of friends and business colleagues. Dave was completely shocked. We recently celebrated 50 years of marriage, and the day of that party remains one of the only times I've ever pulled off a surprise for my husband.

Soon after, in a small office at DCI, located in the Fifth Third Bank Tower, I got to work developing the business case for Cincinnati Works while Dave organized DCI and hired his staff.

Although we'd both served on dozens of nonprofit boards (and even chaired several of them), neither Dave nor I had ever run our own show in the nonprofit world. We figured the more help we had, the better. One of the first things we did was to put together an advisory committee. During the startup phase we identified several nonprofits that we thought would make good partners in our quest to help the poor. We were eager to learn from those who had been in the trenches and to connect with possible partners for the future. The year we started shaping our concept there were more than 90 jobs programs in Cincinnati. We invited the directors of three of these programs with missions similar to ours to serve on our advisory committee.

From the beginning, our desire was to collaborate—not compete—with any person or organization committed to eliminating poverty. Alone we could not possibly provide all the assistance our members would need to overcome their barriers to employment. Joining forces made sense to us, especially with the other poverty-to-work programs in our community.

We soon learned how naïve we were in our thinking. While some on our advisory committee generously gave their time and expertise, we were dismayed when we became suspicious that others had agreed to serve for the sole purpose of monitoring our progress. Their intention did not appear to be to aid Cincinnati Works' success; rather, they seemed concerned about the risk of community money being siphoned away from their own programs. It was the first of many experiences from which we learned that serving the people is not always the first priority of poverty programs. Ironically, the organizations that appeared the most concerned about the competition we might pose for funding were the programs that relied on government funding—even though we reiterated time and time again that we weren't interested in accessing any government money.

When the government stepped into the business of helping the poor, churches and communities largely abdicated their responsibility to serve the poor. Since Lyndon Johnson famously declared his War on Poverty in 1964, the number of urban poor has more than doubled. This major shift of the burden to government led our nation down the wrong path. Because the societal ills facing the poor varied drastically from community to community, it was illogical to expect that realistic cures could be prescribed on a national level. There was a reason God commanded His people to take care of the poor around them. We were called to help our neighbors, and that meant helping the poor in our own city.

We were determined not to seek government money for two main reasons. The first reason was that we felt government funding was too limiting. It was available only if you were serving people receiving public assistance. Yet our research revealed that only 40% of people living in poverty in our region were getting any kind of public assistance. Besides, Dave chafed at all the inefficiencies he saw in the government's approach to helping the poor. He had spent his career working with some of our nation's smartest businesspeople and entrepreneurs. Although he encountered bureaucracy in the business world on occasion, nothing matched the maddening bureaucratic morass that engulfed every aspect of trying to help the poor.

"The poor already have enough barriers to overcome without us creating more for them," he groused in his booming voice. "This system is completely broken."

Navigating the dependency system had long since reached the point where it was practically a full-time job for those intrepid souls attempting to fully avail themselves of it. Even a little dollop of help required filling out endless forms and traipsing from agency to agency.

We also believed that welfare was the single most significant contributing factor in the collapse of the family. It drove the men out of the home. If you were married, you couldn't get support. The more children you had, the more support you got. The government's rules about who could get help contributed—in a big way—to poverty becoming a single mom issue. Fewer than 10% of married women with children ever live in poverty. Forty percent of white, single women with children live in poverty. And an incredible 70% of black, single women with children live in poverty.

Generally, the systems in place were set up to serve women with dependent children. Yet gaping holes ravaged the so-called safety net even for that group, which the government recognized as the most vulnerable and therefore the most vital to serve. Part of government funding was prescriptive in nature, and the prescription wasn't working. It was a prescription for a cold when the patient had pneumonia. The government funding for workforce development rewarded job placements rather than economic self-sufficiency.

Men fared even worse. While we were in the planning stages, rules changed that made it even more difficult to help men in poverty if we accepted public funds. The rare exception was the single father with custody of a minor child. If you were unfortunate enough to be a poor man, you had virtually no place to turn. Women who did not have children, whose children were grown, or who did not have custody of their minor children were largely ineligible for aid. The government's narrow focus on women with dependent children meant only about 40% of the poor in our community were eligible to benefit from the government-funded agencies intended to help them find jobs and get assistance.

Dave and I wanted to help the poor, period. We did not want to be shackled by bureaucratic government rules dictating to whom we could lend a hand. The idea that, if we accepted government money, we could not freely assist everyone living in poverty who was willing to work and capable of doing so made no sense to us whatsoever.

The second reason we didn't want to involve government in our plans was the bureaucratic rules you had to follow if you accepted funding. Accepting government funding meant filling out reams of paperwork and documenting, documenting, documenting. We welcomed accountability, but we wanted the freedom to change our program at any time, in any way that enabled us to better serve the poor. Being forced to get permission from an outside entity that was not part of our community in order to respond to the changes our organization needed to make was unacceptable to us. Besides, the evidence was irrefutable that many existing government programs not only were costly, they simply were not working. Worse, as discussed above, they often had the unfortunate and unintended consequence of marginalizing males in poverty, which contributed to the breakdown of the family unit.

Since 80 cents of every dollar spent to help the poor go to work comes from the government, our decision meant we had cut ourselves off from the primary money pot. Our refusal to accept government money left us solely reliant on private donors and the business community.

Dave and I also noticed that an inordinate amount of available resources were concentrated on the poor who suffered from addiction and/or serious mental illness. That concentration of the funding left only a small sliver of the pie for the poor who we believed had a stronger, more realistic chance of making the transition to work if they were given proper ongoing support.

We had no interest in becoming just another pit stop on the path to yet another failure for poor people who had already experienced layers upon layers of disappointments, traumas, rejections, and humiliation—sometimes at the hands of the very people who were supposed to help them. Dave and I were single-minded about getting as close as we could to creating a one-stop safe haven where the poor could get the training and support they needed as individuals in order to tackle a plethora of barriers while getting a decent job with health benefits.

One of the first orders of business for our advisory committee was to help us formulate our mission statement and goals. Coming up with the bold vision for Cincinnati Works was a snap: Dave and I shared the dream of eliminating poverty in our community. In retrospect, that lofty goal may have kept people from taking us seriously at times. But to us, the vision was always crystal clear.

After three months, the committee established four goals, which were:

- To enable those in poverty to become economically self-sufficient and take control of their lives.
- To meet employers' demand for productive and reliable entry-level workers in the Cincinnati region.
- To save taxpayer dollars by systematically reducing the number of people receiving public assistance.
- To become the catalyst among the jobs programs in the Cincinnati region for systematically reducing the number of people living in poverty by 1–3% annually.

All of these goals seemed reasonable.

The mission statement, the heartbeat of our organization, did not come easily. We, along with the advisory committee, spent weeks agonizing over the wording. We wanted these components reflected in our mission statement:

- We would not give jobs to people. We would assist them to become qualified candidates.
- Our focus would be on people living in poverty.

- We would help people to get a job and retain that job.
- The jobs would be sufficient to lead to economic self-sufficiency.
- We would only work with people who were willing to go to work.
- We would only work with people who would be capable of getting a job with some coaching from us.

The words *willing* and *capable* sparked the most discussion, but Dave and I were adamant that those words be included in the mission statement. Finally, we arrived at something that everyone liked:

Cincinnati Works will partner with all willing and capable people living in poverty to assist them in advancing to economic self-sufficiency through employment.

My first real challenge was to write a business case for Cincinnati Works. As a teacher, I knew how to write a lesson plan. But a business case? That was a different story.

When I sought help from Dave, who had spent decades helping organizations with business plans, he told me to go to the library.

"Liane, I've got to focus on putting together the funding," he said.

Fiscally conservative, Dave wisely insisted that we have operating capital for three years on hand before we ever opened our doors. He set a target of raising $1.8 million for the startup, budgeting $600,000 annually.

"Too many nonprofits are underfunded," he said. "Their staffs worry about whether they're going to get a paycheck on Friday. I want our staff to focus on their work—helping poor people get and keep jobs—not on when their next check will come. We also owe it to our members, who are members for life, to be adequately funded so we can meet their future needs."

At first I was miffed that Dave wouldn't help me put together the business case, especially when I found many examples of how to write a for-profit business case, but not much on nonprofits. At times I felt the dream was becoming a nightmare! But, after struggling, shedding a tear or two, and seeking input from many sources, I finally pulled together an outline with help from two of our advisory committee members—a marketing person from Procter & Gamble and a local attorney. Only after I completed the process did Dave reveal why he insisted I do it without his help.

"I wanted you to own it," he said. "My entire career has been in the business world, and yours has been in education. It would be too easy for me to take the lead. I want us to be equal partners in this."

Throughout our marriage, I often felt like Dave believed in me even more than I believed in myself. Although I was mad at him at times for leaving me alone to muddle through this process, I saw the wisdom in it. And I have to admit, I was proud of the end product.

Dave brought the same energy and focus to fund raising that he'd demonstrated throughout his career with Arthur Andersen. He threw himself into endless rounds of meetings with members of the business community, enthusiastically sharing our mission and how we planned to accomplish it. Like most startup nonprofits, we fiercely competed for a sliver of the charitable contributions that flowed in Cincinnati.

Dave's involvement in the community as both a volunteer and a business leader opened many doors, but he still had to convince potential funders that supporting Cincinnati Works would be a wise investment in a program we hoped would be effective. His ability to make a good business case for our startup, coupled with his reputation, helped garner startup contributions from AT&T, Procter & Gamble, Arthur Andersen, and Arthur Andersen Partners—many of them payable over a three-year period.

One of the clients Dave had become close to when he was with Arthur Andersen was Clay Mathile, who owned and chaired The Iams Company, a pet food manufacturer and distributor. When Dave retired, Clay asked him to a meeting because he wanted Dave on The Iams Company board.

From the first time they met in the early 1980s, Dave and Clay often had deep conversations about how to leave a legacy and make the last years of your life meaningful. Along with many other common values and interests we shared with Clay and his wife, Mary, Dave and I were unswerving in our commitment to leaving our world a better place for the next generation.

Dave made the quick trip to Dayton to meet with Clay in his office at The Iams Company headquarters. After Clay extended the seat on the board and Dave accepted, Dave laid out our idea for him.

"Dave, one of the things I like about you is that you are one of the only men I know who loves measuring things to make sure they work as much as I do," Clay said after Dave finished his presentation and they had discussed several of our ideas at length. "We're constantly bombarded with requests for funding from nonprofits, but hardly any of them use metrics to track whether what they are doing is actually working. If you can develop a model that truly helps the poor, you and Liane will have really done something. You can count on me." Clay and Mary had established a family foundation so that they and their five adult children could give responsibly in a strategic way that delivered the most bang for the buck. Clay and Mary were so concerned about the lack of fiscal understanding and failure to deliver on promises among the leadership of nonprofits that they had set up an intensive two-day training course that nonprofit executives could attend for $100.

"There are a lot of goodhearted people out there, but they have no idea how to set goals and meet them," Clay said. "We want to help them."

The Mathile Family Foundation gave Dave a check for $100,000 that day, with the promise of another $100,000 a year for the next two years. Dave and I were ecstatic that we had received such a big vote of confidence from a smart entrepreneur like Clay.

A point of contention arose within our advisory committee over whether we should seek funding from United Way of Cincinnati. In the mid-1990s our business community supported United Way to the tune of approximately $50 million annually, making it one of the leading sources of funding. Of course, nonprofits lined up for that money. When we started up, about 100 organizations were receiving United Way funding.

Having United Way's support was equivalent to a charity getting the *Good Housekeeping* seal of approval. The downside? Many major corporate donors who supported United Way through annual campaigns in our region refused to further fund a charity already on United Way's roster on the basis that it would be "double dipping."

Most of our advisory committee members thought it was far too early to approach United Way. After all, we were the new kids on the block and had no track record. However, Dave hatched a unique idea that he thought would net us United Way support, hold us accountable for our results, and give us the instant credibility of having United Way's stamp of approval. He met with United Way's executive director and made his pitch. "We want you to give us funding based on a contract," said Dave. He asked for $700 for every member to be paid in this manner: one third when the member got a job, one third after the person was on the job for six months, and the final third when the member had held the job for one year. To our knowledge no other nonprofit had ever proposed such an idea. After several months, United Way notified us that we would be awarded a contract based on our measurable outcomes.

Almost daily Dave girded himself for another round of fund raising, patiently explaining over and again at breakfasts, lunches, dinners, and meetings all over town how our nonprofit poverty-to-work employment agency would differ from the other 90+ welfare-to-work programs in Greater Cincinnati. Although Dave was officially retired, I teased him that you'd never know it to look at him.

"You're still wearing the same uniform you wore when you were at Arthur Andersen," I said one day as he straightened his tie.

"Oh, no, Liane, you're wrong. I never would have worn this color tie or a jacket with a pattern or a button-down shirt," he wisecracked. "Don't you remember? The uniform was a dark suit with a blue or white French-cuffed shirt and a power-red tie."

CHAPTER 2

A White Man in a Suit

*"Dreams are but thoughts
until their effects be tried."*
—William Shakespeare

As I structured Cincinnati Works, Dave and I realized it was difficult to create a program when we didn't know much about our potential clients. He was concerned that "a white man in a suit" would not be able to gain the trust of our potential participants.

We needed to do more research. We wanted to know what would attract someone in poverty to Cincinnati Works, what kind of assistance was needed, and what barriers might keep someone from working. Luckily, the director of Hamilton County Jobs and Family Services came to our aid. He introduced us to several of his employees who were working their way out of poverty.

"The police stop you at least once a week?" Dave asked, incredulous at what he'd just heard.

Alphonso, a late arrival to our roundtable discussion on what it's like to be poor, explained that he missed his bus because a police officer stopped him for questioning.

"Oh, yeah, it happens all the time," said Alphonso, a tall, gangly 20-something, shrugging his shoulders. "I guess they don't like the way I look or something. Ain't no big deal."

Dave and I spent the next two hours with eight young African-American men, all of whom worked at the Department of Human Services. They stood at the precarious precipice between grinding poverty and the edge of self-sufficiency. We peppered them with questions, trying to get an understanding of their concerns, problems, hopes, and dreams. Sensing that our concern was genuine, they eagerly opened up and gave us answers.

The thought of being stopped over and over again by the police simply for walking in your own neighborhood haunted Dave. "No wonder there's so much anger and so little regard for authority," he said later that night as we sat down to dinner. "When we're in trouble, we call the police for help. Based on their experiences, they see the police as harassers."

In the several months following Dave's retirement, we met in small groups with countless poor people from all different age groups and ethnicities in our community. Although research was vital to give us direction, Dave and I wanted firsthand knowledge of the poor we planned to serve. What we encountered was the opposite of suspicion. People eagerly told us their stories. Poor people were used to being ignored, treated as if they were invisible. They longed to be heard and had plenty of ideas about what would help them improve their lives. Race didn't make any difference once they decided our motives were pure and we genuinely cared.

Besides the harassment that people in poor communities experienced at the hands of the police, we got a glimpse of the low self-esteem the poor suffered. Many exhibited symptoms of clinical depression. Unfortunately, the label "lazy" was often placed on poor people in order to explain away the symptoms of depression. We found that perception to be resoundingly false. Most of the poor people we met with were far from lazy. Every day was a struggle and required constant problem solving. Tasks that seemed automatic and simple for us required a lot of energy for them: getting to and from work without a car, finding groceries and paying for them without a paycheck, cashing a paycheck—if you had one—without a bank account.

We also learned that the underground economy represented survival for many. For example, some women bartered hairstyling, while some men bartered car repair. Money rarely changed hands, and that which did was cash only. Suspicion ran deep regarding the trouble that might come from "being on the books."

Most striking of all, we started to grasp the depth of people in poverty's despair and frustration at trying and failing repeatedly to get jobs. Part of the problem stemmed from a lack of experience with the expectations of the job market. The feeling that employers were "out to get them" and anger at a perceived lack of respect was palpable in the room whenever Dave and I met with the poor. A whiff of "disrespect" was accepted as a reasonable cause to quit a job, no matter the consequences.

The actions that some people took often proved self-sabotaging, and upon first blush these actions seemed completely irrational to us. But this battle wasn't about what we thought about their behavior. Dave and I are practical Midwesterners, the children of hardworking blue collar parents who survived the Great Depression. Although Dave grew up poor and my family was on the brink, we knew our own experiences didn't translate.

We harbored no grand illusions that we were going to magically conjure up solutions for problems that had been entrenched in our community for decades. The issues were too complex, the problems too layered for instantaneous results. Most importantly, it all came down to the will of each person in poverty—the individual's resolve to keep striving to move ahead, despite the odds.

From the beginning our aim was to assist people who were willing and able to find and retain jobs. The answers were there in the hearts and minds of the people we wanted to help. We just needed to crack the code.

Throughout 1995 I worked out of Downtown Cincinnati, Inc.'s office, but as our funding goal started to become a reality, the time finally came to conduct a search for a separate Cincinnati Works office. An article on Dave's role with DCI and our dreams for Cincinnati Works ran in *The Cincinnati Post* in October of that year. The story caught Beth Smith's eye. For several years she had been doing sales and marketing for her husband, a world-renowned architectural wood carver. Prior to that she had worked for 15 years as a registered nurse in oncology and emergency room healthcare.

She called me at the DCI office and introduced herself.

"I'm really intrigued with what you're doing," she said.

"We're still in the startup phase," I replied.

Beth asked a lot of good questions. Her enthusiasm for our mission came through in the course of that 15-minute phone call. I wasn't even considering hiring anyone at that point, but before we hung up, I said, "Send me your resume."

Over the next several months, Beth called about once a month to check on our progress.

———⬡⬡⬡———

Dave found an available room at Queen City Vocational Center, which was a part of Cincinnati Public Schools. He brought our cause to the attention of the members of the Cincinnati Board of Education. The board agreed that our mission was worthwhile and shared Dave's hope that some of our job seekers would be funneled into vocational courses. We were granted 1,500 square feet of the building pro bono.

Queen City Vocational Center stood across from Taft High School, located on the fringe of a historic downtown area known as Over-the-Rhine. On the other corner was a police station. Settled by German craftsmen, wealthy businessmen, and poor immigrants in the mid-1800s, this district thrived during a brief period when our city ranked as the second largest in the nation. Over-the-Rhine's bustling population topped 100,000 by 1860.

By the time we opened our doors in February 1996, the population had dwindled to less than 5% of that. The primary inhabitants were African Americans who had been enmeshed in poverty for generations. What had once been handsome, three- to five-story single-family homes in a century gone by had morphed into public housing or stood boarded up, forgotten.

Thanks to the bland architecture popularized in the 1960s, the building where we set up shop looked about as welcoming as a concrete bunker. But, I reminded myself as I pulled into the parking lot nearby, the rent was free. Besides, I figured, the vocational school setting would help us do job training.

Because of three factors—Dave and I were both dollar-a-year volunteers, we used DCI's infrastructure during startup, and the free rent on our new office space—we had virtually no administrative overhead. That made Dave's fund-raising job easier because donors understood that their money would go directly to benefiting the job seekers.

As we interviewed candidate after candidate for the executive director's position, we became uncomfortable making the decision alone because of some of the biases of our advisory committee. We sought the services of a recruiting firm and, on the firm's recommendation, hired a woman who had expertise as a corporate trainer.

The two remaining duties to be done were hiring staff and putting together the curriculum for the job readiness workshop. We hired a consultant to develop a sample curriculum, and my mind kept going back to Beth Smith. Her persistence had greatly impressed me, so I invited her in for an interview. We hired Beth as our job developer.

Part of what we thought would differentiate our approach from many other jobs programs was the way we handled potential employers. We considered potential employers to be clients who were every bit as important to our organization as the poor who were seeking jobs. Our model called for partnering with the business community to help solve a critical issue facing many businesses: reducing turnover and filling jobs at the unskilled entry level. Too often jobs programs had sent the message to businesses that they needed to hire the poor as an altruistic act, rather than working with the person in poverty to make sure that the job seeker was legitimately qualified and prepared for the work world. We didn't expect employers to do Cincinnati Works members any favors—just to give them a chance.

Beth projected warmth without seeming too soft. She tackled her assignment with creativity, enthusiasm, and a genuine desire to understand both what the employers needed and the barriers the poor were up against.

"What do you want our people to know?" she'd ask potential employers. "What are the biggest mistakes job seekers make? What is important to you? What do they need to do in order to succeed in your business?" We emphasized to potential employers that we offered a genuine solution by producing well-prepared candidates.

Despite the research that showed plenty of entry-level job openings in our area, we were deeply concerned that our number of members would quickly swamp the number of jobs that were actually available.

Beth was a workhorse, adept at jumping in wherever she was needed: job coach, recruiter, and, of course, as job developer, the position for which she was hired. Plus, she was completely sold on our deep belief that even the most troubled person could soar if you gave them wings and helped support them. Maybe it was all those years she spent as a nurse, seeing some people buckle under while others recovered. Whatever it was, Beth innately understood our philosophy, which underpinned everything we did. We wanted to teach people to fish—not just give them fish.

Our newly hired executive director determined that most of the curriculum designed by the consultant was impractical and uninformed about the needs of the poor, and she scrapped it. Starting over, she devised a new and improved job readiness curriculum from scratch. The first job readiness workshop started on April 22, 1996, with 26 men and women. It was in session 30 hours per week for three weeks. Channel 9 ran a clip on the first class and posted our phone number, which brought in a few additional job seekers.

We started Cincinnati Works thinking that our biggest challenge would be getting employers to use our services. We never dreamed that recruiting willing and capable participants would prove to be the real key challenge. Getting the word out to our potential clients was our main focus those first several months. The metro bus manager gave us ad space on strips inside the city buses, and we purchased ad space in *The Cincinnati Enquirer.*

It wasn't long, however, before we discovered that pounding the pavement was the most effective tool for spreading the word. During our first few months of operation, Dave and I drove into downtown Cincinnati on Saturday mornings, armed with pamphlets about Cincinnati Works. First we and a few staff members fanned out in Findlay's Farmers Market, which attracted a steady stream of customers from the surrounding neighborhoods. We shook hands, talked to people about what we were doing, and tried to overcome the skepticism that we could sense in most of the people we approached. As the crowds thinned out by mid-morning we walked the streets, talking to small groups gathered on the corners or hanging out on building stoops.

When summer came we had a booth at the Black Family Reunion, a popular annual event held downtown, and hoped to find interested candidates. Although we found some women willing to give our service a try, the men we approached were dubious. Generally they shrugged their shoulders and looked beyond us when we explained what we had to offer. Men also didn't have the time or resources to sit in class for 30 hours.

Our recruiter Nancy Parker was determined to get men into the workshop. She'd walk up to a group of men and boldly announce: "I'm looking for a few good men." Despite these tactics, we were lucky in the beginning if one out of every 10 participants in our workshops was a man.

One scorching summer afternoon I drove over from DCI, where I still had an office, to our new location. My heart leapt when I turned down the street and saw lines of people standing on the sidewalk outside of our building. My mind raced as I tried to imagine what we had done that had finally generated so much interest among job seekers.

I hurriedly parked my car and rushed toward the scene. I spotted Beth in the sea of unfamiliar faces. "What's going on?" I asked.

"A fire drill for the building," she called out above the din of the small crowd.

I should have known better. Nothing about helping the poor comes fast or easy.

CHAPTER 3

Barriers: Nobody Has Just One

"The world is moved along, not only
by the mighty shoves of its heroes,
but also by the aggregate of the tiny
pushes of each honest worker."
–Helen Keller

When Dave and I created Cincinnati Works, we knew that critical to our success would be how well we helped job seekers address their barriers to employment. The 18 months we spent researching the issues facing the working poor and chronically unemployed taught us that every one of the people we sought to help had some barrier keeping them from finding a decent job. What we failed to anticipate was that almost every one of them ran up against multiple barriers. Nobody had just one.

Initially, we felt ill-equipped to deal with the overwhelming complexity of each individual's situation. There was no simple answer to the question some of our wealthy and middle class acquaintances lobbed at us whenever we told them about our retirement plan to devote the rest of our lives to helping poor people become financially stable: "Why don't they just get a job?"

That question made my blood boil, but I reminded myself over and over again that many wealthy and middle class people have not examined the myths that shroud what it means to be poor in America. They simply didn't understand the grit and determination it took to go from being unemployed and subsisting on $9,000 or less per year to earning more than $18,000 per year—200% of the government-defined poverty level, and the amount that we identified as the minimum a person needed to be economically self-sufficient in Greater Cincinnati.

Shirley Smith walked into the space we'd been granted in the Queen City Vocational Center. She bore that frozen look I'd come to know in the eight months since our first job readiness workshop in April. On that Monday before Thanksgiving she sat with six other people, quietly waiting her turn to tell her story to the recruiter. Her eyes downcast, she shifted uneasily in the chair.

"I'm here because you were on the list," she said, her voice barely above a whisper, referring to the fact that we were one of the job readiness agencies approved by the county and were therefore on the list given to her by her case manager. Like many of our early members, Shirley had been forced into action by newly legislated welfare reform, which installed time limits and work mandates for welfare recipients in 1996. Hailed by many as a watershed piece of legislation that would jolt people out of the dependency trap, the reform was a game changer for about 40% of the poor we were working to serve.

Almost overnight, agencies that had been taking government funding for job training changed course and advertised their services as facilitating welfare-to-work. They targeted the same former welfare recipients we were trying to help, but not much had changed in their approach—just the signs on their doors. It was business as usual. Those agencies collected a check from the government in exchange for placing a certain number of people in jobs. But there was little to no follow-up to find out how those placed in jobs were faring in those jobs. Moving from the welfare rolls to the workforce was, for most, like being plopped in the middle of a foreign country where you can't speak the language, read the signs, understand the culture, or obtain the right currency.

Behind Shirley's glasses her dark eyes revealed a wariness and weariness from too many years caught in the dehumanizing cycle of our dependency culture—years spent filling out endless forms in airless rooms to get each little bit of help. In a sense, this mother of two teenage daughters, one in her first year of college and one in middle school, had been frozen. When she came to us that summer, Shirley had not worked at a paying position in more than a decade. A week shy of her high school graduation in 1977, the B-average student capitulated to the pleas of her high school boyfriend, ditched her plans for college, and eloped with him. By the time she reached age 24, she had joined the swelling ranks of single moms, a group five times as likely as married mothers to be in poverty. Besides her 4-year-old daughter, Shirley was pregnant and had taken in her 5-year-old brother when their mother passed away.

Child support never came from her estranged husband. Soon she was hounded by collection agencies. First the electricity was shut off. Next to go was water. Then their comfortable three-bedroom house in Northside went into foreclosure.

Shirley was gripped by severe panic attacks on an almost daily basis. After getting public assistance, she moved her toddler, her newborn daughter, and her brother to a cramped two-bedroom apartment in public housing in College Hill, a racially diverse neighborhood on the northern edge of Cincinnati. Tenant-based assistance paid her rent of $25 a month. For the three children, including her younger brother, Shirley was awarded about $200 a month in food stamps. She felt humiliated standing in the grocery store when she handed the cashier the food stamps.

By the end of the month, they were barely scraping by. Making the money last was almost impossible, no matter how Shirley budgeted. She scrounged for clothing for the kids at Goodwill and the Free Store while often forgoing even the basics for herself. The fog of depression settled in. Many days Shirley struggled to think of a single reason to get out of bed. "My apartment felt safe," said Shirley. "I didn't want to face the world. Caseworkers treated me as less than human. I felt like just another cog in the machine."

Once her girls and younger brother were all in elementary school, she volunteered in the school library and their classrooms to keep busy and be close to them. She loved to read and do research. She taught herself to type. When she was immersed in a project, she could forget about her circumstances for a few hours. The years passed, and Shirley continued to volunteer, but when the new legislation brought her to Cincinnati Works, she was convinced no one would hire her. She came to us with virtually no work history and no special skills.

"What do you think you have to offer an employer?" asked Beth, whose 15 years of experience as a registered nurse gave her the perfect mix of empathy, practicality, and calm in crisis. Her serene nature had a soothing effect on our members.

"Nothing that I can think of," Shirley replied, shrugging her shoulders. Beth waited patiently for her to continue. After a few moments Shirley murmured, "I've been a stay-at-home mom. I like to write and research things, and I've volunteered a lot at my daughters' school and in the community."

"That's a good start," said Beth. "You may not have work skills, but you've got life skills that would be valuable to an employer."

Shirley relaxed slightly and smiled for the first time that day. During the course of the interview, Beth learned that Shirley was anything but the stereotypical welfare mom. She told me later that it was the first of many lessons she learned at Cincinnati Works. "You've got to really listen to people's individual and unique stories," Beth said.

Shirley shyly told Beth that she had written a book about Mozart and had become an expert on the Beatles' music and history during the time she spent at home.

"Why don't you bring me a copy of your book?" Beth asked. "I'd love to read it."

Despite her trepidation, Shirley signed up for the next available job readiness workshop, offered the following week, and became part of Class #7. We had whittled the workshop down to two weeks by that time because job seekers were in dire straits when they came to us. They were anxious to get to work, so three weeks wasn't practical, and we were losing potential job seekers as a result.

In the interim, before the next workshop started, Shirley went to the Hamilton County Department of Jobs and Family Services. There she joined others who were unemployed in a room where they spent the days dutifully looking through newspapers for job leads and writing down possibilities.

No one met with them individually to give any support or guidance.

After Shirley successfully completed our two-week job readiness workshop, we sent her to our partner, Dress for Success, where she picked out clothes and accessories for her interviews. We gave her a bus card so that she could get to and from interviews. She was insecure about her lack of computer skills, but in the workshop she had learned to make the most of her experience as a volunteer.

"I never thought I was lazy," Shirley said. "I just didn't think I had any skills that would be of value to an employer." Thankful to find people who genuinely cared about her, she insisted on volunteering in our office. After a six-week job search, she landed a $6-an-hour position as a file clerk in the library room of Fifth Third Bank, a bus ride away from her College Hill apartment. She shyly rang the cowbell that we'd brought into the office, a remnant of Dave's Arthur Andersen days. Every person who found a job got to ring the bell to announce that their job search had concluded successfully.

Knowing that we stood behind her and that she represented Cincinnati Works, Shirley made it a goal to be 15 minutes early to work every day. "I hate being late," she said. Shirley was overwhelmed at first by everything about being in the work world—the size of the bank, the challenge of remembering all that she had to remember, being on her feet all day, and dealing with her boss and coworkers. Beth stayed in close contact with Shirley, allaying her fears. Shirley regularly attended our monthly alumni support group.

Then came the day when she was confronted by a pending cut in her housing benefit and the mound of paperwork that earning wages for the first time in 12 years had triggered. That's just another way the system appeared to be almost stacked against the poor. As soon as they began to make progress in their struggle to get out of poverty, the few support systems and safety nets they relied upon were removed. The perverse effect was that the poor were penalized for working. The precariousness of people's journeys out of poverty became painfully evident at this juncture where their employment meant they either wound up about where they started, or they fell behind, depending on which benefits had been cut off. Our job was to convince them to hang on and keep fighting.

Shirley called Beth, distraught and filled with doubts. "Can I really do this?" she asked, her voice quavering and barely audible.

"Shirley, your employer absolutely loves you. You are doing an excellent job," said Beth. "You are definitely going to make it."

Ever probing, and looking for the numbers to back up decisions and actions, Dave kept seeking proof that the poor who were going through the job training programs that had popped up all over town were actually getting jobs and keeping them. "In God I trust—everybody else I audit," Dave was fond of saying.

Time after time, agencies purporting to help the poor find jobs refused to provide us with any numbers or hard evidence of their effectiveness. Dave's repeated requests were either met with lame excuses of why the numbers weren't tracked, or with stony silence. They weren't offering any real solutions to the many barriers the poor face when trying to obtain employment.

Most of these agencies were chasing government money and getting paid for putting people in jobs with little accountability regarding how long a person remained employed. Practically all of the other welfare-to-work programs in town viewed us as competition, pure and simple, and though we found little success in trying to partner with agencies that claimed to be helping job seekers, one of our most successful partnerships was formed prior to startup.

During the process of benchmarking other programs, we became aware of many legal barriers facing the population we would be serving, but Dave and I had no idea of the extent of this barrier until we had been open for a few months. We discovered that more than 50% of the job seekers had some kind of legal issue. Early on we added a staff position with legal expertise to meet the need. Our legal advocate helped people resolve legal issues and assisted them in navigating the intimidating legal system. Having someone on our staff who helped in this capacity went a long way toward mitigating the fear of legal authorities that many of our members brought with them.

Dave approached Mary Asbury, the executive director of Legal Aid of Cincinnati, to serve on our legal advisory committee, which included a criminal defense attorney and representatives from the Hamilton County Sheriff's Office, Hamilton County Municipal Court, Hamilton County Drug Court, Hamilton County Probation Department, Hamilton County Public Defender's Office, and Frost, Brown, and Todd, a local law firm.

Legal Aid's mission overlapped ours: We both promoted self-sufficiency. When legal issues remained unaddressed, the poor either failed to get jobs in the first place or cycled rapidly through a series of jobs.

When a job seeker came to Cincinnati Works, we required a criminal background check. We worked with job seekers who had been convicted of misdemeanors and nonviolent felonies because some of our employers would accept employees with these kinds of offenses on their criminal records. Every applicant's criminal background check was reviewed privately with the individual on the second day of the workshop to check for errors and probation compliance. If a person had an open arrest warrant or a violent felony on his or her record, that person was not allowed to continue the workshop. However, since we made that clear during screening, we rarely had anyone in the workshop whose background check raised a problem.

The poor regularly relied on unscrupulous, self-designated "street" lawyers for advice and, as a result, made egregious errors when dealing with the legal system. For instance, many were unaware that failing to appear in court for a misdemeanor charge could lead to one being arrested, put in jail, and charged with a felony.

We also made sure job seekers' expectations regarding prospective employers were in line with reality. For example, healthcare providers and financial institutions were legally bound to follow stringent rules about whom they could and couldn't hire. We helped job seekers understand that these additional rules weren't personal. We redirected those who had criminal records to employers with more inclusive hiring policies. During the workshop we carefully instructed job seekers on how to properly and honestly fill out an application, and we coached them on how to talk about their criminal records during a job interview.

Legal Aid provided free legal help for the poor and had 600 attorneys, representing 33 firms in Cincinnati, who volunteered their time and the resources of their offices. The nonprofit—which got 30,000 requests for help per year and typically could handle only about 6,000 of those—gave our job seekers preference. "If someone comes from Cincinnati Works, I know that person is typically committed to getting his or her life on track," said Mary Asbury.

We did not expect employers to treat our job seekers as charity cases. All we asked from them was that our people be given equal consideration. From the get-go we had concentrated on helping the job seekers meet the needs of the market. We never expected businesses to lower their standards. As a matter of fact, we told employers that if they had better applicants, they should hire those candidates rather than Cincinnati Works members. Our goal was to deliver people to the marketplace who would retain their jobs longer than applicants employers could hire on their own.

"No one has ever gotten or kept a job because we helped them fight an employment rights case," Mary noted, contrasting our approach to that of other social service agencies. "You don't fall for alibis or excuses. You just help the person train for and keep a job."

Legal Aid has guided our members through a whole host of issues, including domestic violence, abuse, custody cases, bad landlords, predatory lenders, bankruptcy, child support issues, and expungements. The latter is a legal way of eliminating a nonviolent felony from a person's record. In Ohio a person is eligible for an expungement on a one-time basis, and only if they have just one nonviolent felony or misdemeanor. It's considered a second chance. Helping a member get an expungement can make a dramatic difference in that person's marketability. We walked members through the complex legal process of sealing a police record. An expungement offered a second chance for people who made an isolated mistake. Strict criteria are used to determine eligibility, and not all requests are granted. (The rules regarding expungements vary widely from state to state.) Sean was fired from a job that he loved when his employer saw a disorderly conduct conviction on his record. Legal Aid assisted him in receiving an expungement. "There are two things I am very proud of," Sean said. "Being able to pass a drug test, and now my police check says 'no criminal or traffic record.' Jobs that require a clean record, I can go apply for those jobs now and not worry about them rejecting me. Also, with a record, people looked at me differently when I went to work, and now I don't get that."

Chuck is a man who, at age 39, decided he wanted to turn his life around. To his dismay he found that his criminal record and history as a drug addict made that almost impossible. By the time he made contact with us at a job fair, his spirits were sagging.

As a member of Class #3, Chuck learned how to speak directly with employers about his past mistakes, accepting responsibility and stating what he had learned. With our help, Chuck landed a job as a cook at a social service agency, and then later in food service at a hotel. After a year on that job, he was promoted to the waitstaff.

We have sometimes found major errors on police records and asked to have them corrected, which dramatically improved that job seeker's chances of getting a job. Often workshop attendees started the classes visibly sad or angry, not knowing why their job searches were fruitless. For example, Alice's record was intermingled with someone else's with the same name. Her actual record was clear, but background checks mistakenly returned 15 misdemeanors and one felony. She had spent several months unemployed, struggling to find work. Once we helped clear her name, she quickly found a job.

Among those who ask for legal help, more than 60% of women with dependent children are wrangling with child support issues. That number has continued to escalate as more than one third of our nation's children are now born out of wedlock, including more than 70% of all African-American children.

In countless cases we helped mothers (and occasionally custodial fathers) get started in the child support collection process for the first time. We helped people understand the collection process, connected them to support payers' employers to help stimulate collection, and supported those who wanted to file contempt of court charges to enforce collection. (A person who willfully disobeys a court order to pay child support can be found to be in contempt of court; the accompanying threat of incarceration often serves as a strong motivator to pay.)

The overriding purpose of our child support efforts was to generate an infusion of real cash for the children and families at the highest risk for poverty: single women with children. More than 175,000 children in Greater Cincinnati lived in poverty, and many of them lived with a single parent. Cincinnati Works participated on a community level with the Hamilton County Child Support Planning Committee and the Child Support Outreach Committee, and we partnered with the Hamilton County Justice System and Legal Aid Society.

We helped noncustodial fathers too. Usually that meant supporting the father's stability in the regular employment sector, which increased his chances of staying in the above-ground economy—people in poverty often took jobs that paid cash, off the books, in their struggle to make ends meet—and making his child support payment.

We developed partnerships with employers that allowed us to support an efficient wage-reporting and wage-withholding process. Our relationship with Child Support Enforcement and our thorough understanding of how the system works allowed us to answer members' questions and facilitated a smooth process of collection without scaring the fathers away. Our knowledge helped us walk them through the court process and court appearances. Because of our relationship with the courts, we received referrals from them for fathers who needed help finding employment. We also advocated for members during the hearing process.

Many of our job seekers lived in nontraditional families with unusual situations, which presented challenging legal questions. For example, Tabitha's children's father was in prison for domestic violence against Tabitha. As his release date neared, he repeatedly threatened to take custody of their children away from Tabitha when he was released. Frightened, she called us.

Armed with information from Legal Aid, we assured Tabitha that, as a single mom, she was the sole legal custodian of her children. She was enormously relieved, but the 24-year-old still faced many barriers. She had to make her job her top priority because no one else in her extended family worked. She had to leave her children with a babysitter she didn't know well. Even though she had filed charges against her abusive ex-boyfriend, she still waffled over whether she wanted a relationship with him. She had to share her legal issues with us when she felt uncomfortable talking about them with anyone. She weathered harsh criticism from her mother for moving into her own apartment. She faced the loss of friendships because her time and energy were focused on her job. She had no support from anyone except Cincinnati Works team members. And, as if all that wasn't enough, she had recently found out she was no longer eligible for food stamps because she was working, yet she was not making enough to be self-sufficient. Members battling to become self-sufficient many times found themselves at odds with their own cultures and with the system.

We also frequently supported job seekers in tackling problems involving poor housing and unscrupulous landlords. Lead paint was an issue in many of the century-old houses and apartments in which most of our members resided. Mold, unsafe water, and such other health hazards as rodents and roaches were also common problems. Some landlords ignored the problems as long as they could get away with it. Meanwhile, children and adults developed asthma and other respiratory illnesses that, when the situation escalated, often necessitated a trip to the emergency room, which brought with it medical bills that the family, lacking health insurance, could not pay.

When Olikia's landlord replaced a broken cabinet in her kitchen, she was alarmed to see that the wall behind the cabinet was covered with thick black mold. When she asked the landlord what he was going to do about the situation, he shrugged and proceeded to install the new cabinet over the mold. We contacted the board of health, and we informed the landlord of Olikia's intention to place her rent in escrow until he addressed the mold problem. The landlord responded by moving Olikia to a newer, larger unit without a mold problem.

Childcare, which our job seekers named repeatedly as one of their biggest barriers to steady employment, posed some of the hardest problems to solve. About half of our members were single moms with dependent children. Like most parents, our job seekers generally didn't trust people they didn't know to watch their children and therefore often had difficulty finding reliable providers.

The problem was compounded when an extra bus ride, in addition to the member's commute to work, was needed to get to the childcare provider in the morning and in the evening. Further complicating matters, some providers took only children who fell within specific age ranges. That often meant that two or more providers were needed for each job seeker, requiring valuable hours out of the day to be spent riding the bus. Additionally, a job seeker may need childcare before and after school. Even trickier was that many of the jobs available to our members were second or third shift, further limiting childcare options.

As we tried to assist those who needed childcare, we became baffled by all the various scenarios. Even the seemingly simple task of finding providers within specific geographic areas proved overwhelming for us. We began to truly understand the challenges faced by a single mom trying to do this on her own. Eventually we partnered with 4C for Children, an organization that kept track of quality childcare providers, the ages each provider accepted, and the hours they worked.

Arriving at the office early one morning, I could tell from the tension in our recruiter Nancy's face that she was on a tough call. My office window looked out into the big, open room where the staff worked. The recruiters spent the majority of their days fielding stressful calls—sometimes as many as 30–40 a day—dealing with problems ranging from clashes with employers to breakdowns in the emergency childcare plan. This time, though, Nancy, who had worked in the mental health arena before joining us, appeared shaken. When she finally hung up the phone, she told me that the job seeker on the other end of the line was so distraught that he was threatening to commit suicide.

Many of the toughest barriers job seekers have to overcome are not obvious. A barrier for six in 10 of our job seekers is depression or anxiety, which, in the poor, often is mistaken for laziness or lack of motivation. No one on our staff was professionally qualified to deal with these issues.

People in poverty often fail to recognize their symptoms as mental health problems. Some self-medicate with drugs and alcohol, which yields another set of problems. Few have access to mental health services, and for those who do, an available appointment can be months in the future. Furthermore, in poor communities there is a deep stigma attached to mental illness, so those who might benefit from professional help are less likely to take advantage of it when it is available.

Problem solving is compromised or nonexistent in the crisis mode, and bad decision making becomes a pattern. In spite of our effort to instill the 411 concept—*Call the Cincinnati Works office for information before you quit or at the first sign of trouble*—some of our members still treat our staff like 911 and don't call until they are deeply in crisis. Drama is the status quo, and they are unable to judge when they would benefit from outside intervention.

Many of our members have already experienced failure time and time again, and we do not want to contribute to yet another failure, so we work hard to help them overcome their mental health barriers to employment. Some of the biggest issues that interfere with work are fear, poor self-esteem, lack of self-confidence, poor work ethic, and feelings of powerlessness.

Lack of adequate behavioral skills is another major barrier. Lonnie, a tall, outgoing 19-year-old, worked on the prep line in the kitchen of a chain restaurant for nine months. His skill and fast work soon won him a promotion to head prep cook. The oldest of eight children in a violent household and a high school dropout, Lonnie was proud of his accomplishment and the 25-cent raise that came with it.

Then one night one of his coworkers made a remark about his braids. Lonnie chased her out of the kitchen brandishing a large spatula with a serrated edge. He was fired on the spot, and that incident became a blot on his employment record. In our workshop Lonnie started to grasp why that behavior was unacceptable in the workplace.

Self-sabotage is another destructive behavior that we frequently see. In many cases our members know exactly what they should and need to do, but they elect not to do it and thereby undermine their own success. Inappropriate attitudes also hold people back. A chip on a member's shoulder or a belief that everyone is out to get them can prevent them from finding or keeping employment. An entitled attitude or too much pride can keep them from even seriously looking for a job. All of these internal issues are addressed in the workshop and on an individual basis with Cincinnati Works staff.

Lack of skills and job seekers' inflated views of their skills present another barrier. Most entry-level jobs do not require specific skills, but most do require the interpersonal and other soft skills that we teach in the job readiness workshop. But an inflated self-concept is common and causes some to refuse a job because they think it is beneath them. We help job seekers understand that, for example, if you don't have computer skills, you will not be able to function as an administrative assistant.

Many of our job seekers need to learn new ways to manage conflict. They have to unlearn their usual survival techniques and reactions to conflict—usually escalating the conflict using inflammatory words or even their fists—and learn control through anger management techniques.

Anthony Carson, a flamboyantly dressed 38-year-old, joined us as part of Class #9 in early 1997. He had worked in housekeeping as a nonunion employee with the Federal Reserve for almost 15 years before he was terminated from his $30,000-a-year job in August 1996.

"My new supervisor labeled me a 'hostile employee,'" Anthony said. "He claimed I threatened him. Being fired like that after that many years of service meant no pension, no benefits at all. I fought it to the bitter end, but not being in the union, I didn't have a whole lot of help. You bet I was angry. Some of those folks broke bread in my house."

By the time he came to us, the newlywed had been out of work six months and was "a little down" by his own admission. His niece saw how discouraged he was and told him about Cincinnati Works. Every day of the two-week workshop Anthony came in dressed to the nines, and he often bought lunch for his classmates. He bragged about his 401(k) plan and about the fact that he and his wife, a teacher, owned their home.

"I came in a little cocky, a little full of myself," he admitted. "I had some money saved up. I didn't think I was better than no one else, but I didn't let nothing bother me."

Anthony hadn't been on an interview in years, and despite his bravado, he was nervous. "Beth took me on job interviews and encouraged me," he said. "Cincinnati Works taught me how to talk to employers about the past and how to dress like a gentleman for my interviews. They helped me with my resume. I took what they taught me and ran with it."

Just before Anthony graduated from the workshop, Beth told him about a job opening at a bar at the airport. He applied and was hired. He bused tables and cleaned the restaurant for three weeks. Then, in March 1999, "I felt like I stuck a winning coin in a slot machine," he said.

In one week he got offers from the Aronoff Center for the Arts, the newly renovated Music Hall, and the Regal Hotel. Although the pay at Music Hall was slightly better, at $7.50 an hour, Anthony took the third-shift, union job with Regal because the hotel's benefits package was better. "I wanted to be the best floor tech they'd ever seen," said Anthony. "When they saw how I stripped and waxed floors and took care of the carpet, it didn't take no time for me to move up. Anything I try to do, I try to do it good."

Within nine months he got a 50-cent raise and the title of supervisor. He continued to get raises and promotions, and he's been named employee of the month five times.

"I just needed a little boost," Anthony told Beth. "I know what it's like to work hard." Then he quietly thanked her for helping him learn how to talk about the problem he'd had with his previous employer.

Anthony added with a grin, "And I learned to keep my mouth shut."

Each one of our members is an individual. Our role is to put a little air under their wings—just until they can fly on their own. Some fall to the earth and drop out of sight, but all the effort is worth it when you see the ones who soar.

Barriers to Change

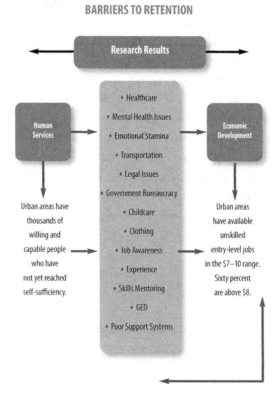

BARRIERS TO RETENTION

CHAPTER 4

Breaking Down Our Own Walls

"Every worthwhile accomplishment, big or little, has its stages of drudgery and triumph; a beginning, a struggle, and a victory."
−Mahatma Gandhi

I could not believe my eyes as I glanced across the room. There, lying on top of her desk, staring straight up at the ceiling, was our receptionist, counting sheep out loud.

"What are you doing?" I asked, incredulous at the spectacle she was causing. I was even more amazed when I noticed that our executive director was sitting in her office, ignoring the whole scene.

The woman, who had come to work that morning wearing an elaborate turban, explained without looking at me that she had had an altercation with another member of our staff.

"This is how I cope," she said, still looking at the ceiling.

We made some real errors in hiring our first staffers. Some oozed empathy but took a social service approach with participants. Instead of viewing job seekers as capable human beings who just needed some help and guidance to learn to get jobs and advance, they fell into the trap of doling out instant fixes, rather than teaching our members how to solve problems for themselves.

Dave and I operated from a modified version of Lao Tzu's proverb: *"Give a man a fish, and you feed him for a day. Teach a man to fish, and you feed him for a lifetime."* Staff members who encouraged dependency were in direct conflict with our desire to help the poor and working poor escape the dependency culture in which many of them had been mired for generations.

A few staffers came with personal agendas and were more concerned with advancing themselves than advancing the job seekers. We discovered that one man who was supposed to be recruiting new members was handing out political flyers promoting himself as a candidate in an upcoming election. The final straw came when our job developer Beth revealed that he had been making inappropriate comments to her.

Others had such poor work habits as excessive absenteeism and conducting personal business while at work, rendering them useless as role models for our members—unless you could count them as examples of "what not to do on the job!" Some even attempted to teach our members by shaming or by demanding adherence to their preconceived solutions.

Dave and I realized we were on a steep learning curve. For Cincinnati Works to work, our staff had to be effective at teaching and modeling work behavior. After less than a year in operation, we essentially cleaned house. This time when we hired people, we didn't look at coming from the social services arena as an asset. Our approach just didn't mesh well with the mindset that was ingrained in those who had spent their careers in social services. We believed in our members and their ability to become self-sufficient. We didn't see them as charity cases or people we needed to fix. We defined our role in their lives as supportive coaches and mentors. In some cases our members might need ongoing support for years, but that still didn't diminish our faith that someday they would stand entirely on their own.

Sometimes the answer is right in front of you. Beth Smith was originally hired as a job developer. Although she was compassionate, she had just enough of a no-nonsense edge to make her effective with the people we wanted to help. We named her interim executive director 14 months after she started with us. She innately understood the mission and shared our passion.

We suspended our advertising campaign in the newspaper. It was expensive and produced few results. Our best advertisements were our members themselves. Word spread quickly in the community that we legitimately offered free help, and we weren't making a buck off of their backs. Although men ignored us initially, the numbers of men in our classes gradually crept up. Cincinnati Works was one of the few resources in the community that was available to them.

Derrick Mayes, 21 years old when he joined us, was seriously depressed. He and a close friend from high school had been working for an asbestos abatement company for a year. It was hard, hazardous work and required him to travel a lot, but Derrick didn't complain. Soon, however, the abatement firm started cheating the young men of their wages and delaying their paychecks. Derrick and his friend also grew concerned that they had not been issued safety gear. Finally they both quit.

Growing up in Lincoln Court, a housing project in downtown Cincinnati, with a single mom and a younger sister, Derrick dreamed of becoming an electrical engineer. After high school graduation, his grade point average garnered him a scholarship, and he qualified for enough additional financial aid to attend Cincinnati State. But, after his first year, an error caused the financial aid office to begin falsely dunning him for a bill he had already paid, and they refused to release his tuition money for the next semester.

Intimidated and uncertain how to resolve the problem, Derrick decided the only thing to do was to drop out of college and take the first job he could find. "I was afraid it was hurting my credit," he said.

Meanwhile, his former high school girlfriend had given birth to his baby girl. The child support he owed her was adding up fast. The pressure built to the point where he could hardly sleep. "I tried to find jobs to help me plant my foot down so I could be a good dad to my daughter," he said.

A low point came one Thanksgiving when the crack addicts living upstairs broke into the efficiency he was renting near University Hospital and stole all his clothes, his television, and his radio. "Then they trashed the house," he said. "I'll never forget coming home and seeing my door hanging open."

His friend and former coworker came by to tell him about a new program called Cincinnati Works. Derrick said he could feel the positive energy the more his friend talked about what he was learning.

"They're like a family. They have their arms open," the friend told Derrick.

Derrick went to the next orientation. He liked what he heard. Besides, he figured he didn't have anything to lose. He joined Class #10 in 1998.

The workshop proved an eye-opener for Derrick. No one had ever talked to him about how to dress for and conduct himself during a job interview, write a resume, or search for a job; no one had ever taken the time to hammer home the importance of being on time and showing up every day.

He met with Legal Aid about collecting back wages from the asbestos abatement company. Most of all, he thrived with the one-on-one attention. Someone listened to him. That was a new experience.

When Derrick completed the workshop, he got a job almost immediately with a structural engineering company that was working on the new Cincinnati Reds baseball stadium. He loved surveying land and reading plots. "I liked being outdoors, working with my hands," he said. "I don't mind getting dirty."

Three months into the assignment, though, he called the office early one morning. Beth answered.

"I'm so glad you're there," said Derrick. "My supervisor's cussing at me. There are racial overtones to everything he says to me. I can't take this anymore."

Beth patiently talked him through the situation, providing tips on how to deal with it without losing his temper. The next time Derrick came by our office, he was elated. "I didn't blow up. That was a big victory," he said.

Soon after, however, the company laid Derrick off. "I was right back in the same situation again with child support adding up and no way to pay it," he said. "I was really down." Derrick didn't give up. He came back to Cincinnati Works, and we once again did what we could to facilitate his job search. He got an interview for a position as a municipal worker for the City of Cincinnati, but he was scared to go to the interview. A little prodding revealed that he was nervous about getting lost on his way. He'd rarely been out of his neighborhood, and since he didn't drive, he was convinced he'd bungle the route and blow his chance. With some encouragement and some route planning, he made it to the interview and got the job making $10 an hour with no benefits. Soon he took on a second job as a security officer with one of our core employers, Securitas, earning $9.50 an hour. In short order he was promoted to supervisor, making $13 an hour.

Glenna Parks, 35, who was recruited right after high school to work for Prudential Health Care and stayed for 17 years, was stunned when she was laid off. She collected unemployment benefits for the first time in her life and remained unemployed for six months. Then she answered a blind newspaper ad for the position of employment coordinator, a new role at Cincinnati Works that would allow the job developer to concentrate exclusively on finding new employers. In addition to her interview with us, she had recently interviewed for positions at two other firms. Within days she had offers from all three organizations.

Beth was impressed by Glenna's energy and her willingness to handle a wide range of tasks. In a place where we all emptied the trash and made our own copies, we didn't suffer anyone who wouldn't do the same. Beth also thought Glenna's own recent experience of hard times would enable her to relate to our members.

In September 1998, Beth hired Glenna to run our job searches and represent us at job fairs. She developed job leads and worked with our members during the job search. She also attempted some follow-up with employers. The economy was booming. "Most observers thought that if you were breathing, you should be able to get hired," recalled Glenna of that time.

However, that simply wasn't true for the people we were serving. There was no booming economy in their neighborhoods. The poor remained mystified by the unspoken rules of the world of employment. Employers were often likewise baffled by the self-sabotaging attitudes and behaviors of people who obviously desperately needed the jobs the employers provided.

Beth developed an idea. She wanted to narrow our focus on employers. Part of Glenna's job became to identify what we came to call "core employers." These employers were more likely to have jobs for our members and to offer decent starting wages and health benefits after a certain length of time on the job. The employers also gave us specifics on issues that would be deal breakers for them—for example, a misdemeanor on a candidate's criminal record. Most importantly, we attempted to build strong relationships with our core employers.

Glenna questioned job seekers more closely to determine if their expectations and interests were well matched to the jobs for which they were applying. For example, if someone had arthritis and couldn't tolerate the cold, we didn't want to send that person to interview for a position as an outdoor security officer. Glenna's charge was to decrease the number of mismatches like this, in which a job seeker was sent out to interview for an unsuitable job, or an employer hired someone who wasn't a good fit.

Then, just two months after we hired her and on the day before Thanksgiving, she was diagnosed with a brain tumor. Her surgery was scheduled for January 11, 1999. Thankfully the tumor turned out to be slow-growing and benign. When Dave and I went for a visit, we arranged for the nun who was the top administrator at Good Samaritan Hospital to come by and pray with Glenna. "Will my job still be there?" she asked us.

"Of course," I told her. "You just concentrate on getting well."

"God put me with you at just the right time," she said.

While Glenna recuperated over the next two months, Beth met Jane Howie, a store manager at Babies "R" Us, at a National Human Resources Association meeting. Looking for a career change, Jane joined us to do marketing and to fill Glenna's role temporarily.

Our initial hiring missteps still fresh in my mind, I was finally starting to feel like we were developing a really solid team.

In almost three years at the bank, our member Shirley Smith never missed a single day of work. Eventually she was promoted to lease operations, and then to customer service, where she interacted with customers at other bank branches and at car dealerships. She was making $7.25 an hour with health benefits.

By June 1999, Shirley wanted more of a challenge. She had continued to attend our alumni meetings, and she contacted Beth, who told her that there was an opening with us for an employment support specialist. This was a position we established to offer ongoing support to our members, help teach classes within the workshops, and help members improve their problem solving skills. She interviewed with Beth.

"I want the opportunity to make a difference in people's lives," Shirley said. "I understand the challenges members face, especially single moms—finding childcare, dropping the kids off, catching buses, and trying to stretch your limited funds. I can give these women the support that I didn't have. Having me here proves that people can do this. They can make their lives better for themselves and their children." The normally introverted Shirley became increasingly animated as she made her case for joining the Cincinnati Works staff.

"I've seen the 'factory approach' spitting unprepared people out into the workforce," she continued. "You don't feel validated in that system. Caseworkers are overworked, short with you, and treat you with suspicion. Here people care about you and what your life is like. The staff here believes in you before you believe in yourself."

We saw in Shirley the kind of commitment to Cincinnati Works principles that we looked for in our job seekers and in our own employees, and we hired her as our newest employment support specialist.

In September 1999, Beth learned that she had Stage I breast cancer. I was stunned when I heard the news. Within one year, two of our staff members had been struck by serious illness, which represented a quarter of our staff. Dave and I had grown to love our staff like family. "We're here for you. Whatever you need," we told Beth.

Despite a brutal schedule of chemotherapy, followed by radiation and 138 doctor appointments over the next several months, Beth took just five sick days. She insisted that being at work was her therapy. With her upbeat attitude and sheer grit, she inspired both the staff and our members. Our members deal with so much trauma in their lives that, in an odd way, the difficulties our staff was facing only seemed to make our members that much more comfortable.

Nobody was putting on a front or pretending that everything always had a happy ending. Yet, at the same time, we just kept showing up to help our members along their way.

Late in 1999, we got some much-needed good news. I had applied for a grant with Bethesda Hospital Foundation outlining our empirical approach to finding jobs in the community for the poor and helping systematically remove their barriers to employment. I explained that 60% of our job seekers suffered from mental health problems or anxiety that kept them from finding work and crippled their ability to stay on the job. The foundation agreed to provide a salary and licensing support to give us a mental health specialist on staff.

"Dave, this is great!" I said. To my knowledge, no other jobs program provided a mental health specialist on-site. We wasted no time interviewing for the position and hired a psychologist.

On a good day, somebody with depression and anxiety can get a job. The problem is that they can't keep the job. A counselor may refer someone to a mental health clinic, but there is a six- to eight-month backlog, and the people won't go. The culture teaches that if you go into those places, you're nuts, you're crazy. The street fools people into self-medicating with illegal drugs and alcohol in order to feel better, but that path just makes the depression worse.

In the attitude and conflict management classes during the workshop, members identified behaviors that have derailed them and inappropriate responses that had become automatic. Changing thinking and behavior patterns took monumental effort and patience.

Besides conflict management, bad attitudes, chronic fatigue, and depression, our mental health counselor dealt with such other issues as:

- Individual, intrapersonal problems, e.g., fear of success or failure, poor self-esteem/self-confidence, anger, and unrealistic expectations of self and others
- Male and female relationship issues
- Marriage problems regarding power, finances, and the distribution of responsibilities
- Abandonment issues and physical and sexual abuse

In addition to teaching in the workshop and meeting with job seekers individually, our counselor helped identify job seekers' mental health problems and determined whether they were beyond our ability to help. In those cases we made a referral to another agency that was better qualified to handle that problem. When we made the judgment as to whether we could assist someone, we always considered whether we knew of any employer who would employ that person after they finished the workshop. If we didn't, it would be misleading and unfair to grant that person Cincinnati Works membership.

After six months we realized that, if our projections based on the numbers served were correct, we'd soon become the largest employer of mental health specialists in the county! The problem was that the psychologist wanted to cure the poor he was seeing with long-term therapy. Our immediate goal, however, was to get them stable enough to be productive in the workplace. There was a yawning chasm between providing ongoing, long-term mental health care and giving members enough help to produce stability. We were at cross-purposes. Our goal was to provide brief, employee assistance-style counseling and refer those with more profound, long-term therapy needs to community mental health services.

After almost three years of operation, with the number of job seekers failing to mushroom like we'd hoped, we faced the fact that our location was hindering our growth. Transportation issues were keeping potential job seekers from coming to us in the first place.

Even though we were technically downtown, we were situated on the outskirts. Our research showed that many job seekers took two different buses or more to reach us. Like many cities, Cincinnati's bus service is designed around a hub and spoke system, which is convenient for the operator but not for the people who use the system.

One snowy morning I made the 30-minute drive to the office from our house in the suburbs only to find the building's doors locked. A few other staffers, who also usually arrived early, were standing outside too.

"What's going on?" I asked.

"Cincinnati Public Schools are shut down for a snow day," Beth said.

I couldn't believe it. I could feel my face flush. Once again we were locked out of the building and our offices. The building was only available according to the Cincinnati Public Schools' schedule. Even on regular workdays we found ourselves at the mercy of the janitors who controlled the keys. Some days they would demand that we vacate the building because they wanted to close early. Or they'd disrupt a workshop by running noisy cleaning machinery in the cavernous room where we were located. Staying at the office to catch up on work past 4 p.m. was out of the question because of the janitorial staff's desire to lock up and go home.

Communicating the erratic schedule of our building's availability to potential job seekers proved impossible. My heart pounded in my chest as I thought about job seekers spending precious bus fare to come all the way to our offices only to find them closed.

"How many people have we lost?" I asked Dave, boiling with frustration at the thought of some single mom going to all the trouble to get to us and then feeling like she'd hit another dead end. "We've got to change this now."

The scheduling issues also did nothing to aid our mission to help job seekers understand the importance of timeliness and consistency in the workplace. How could we hope to communicate the rules of business in corporate America when we were unable to model a business environment for job seekers and members in our own office?

We came to understand that our location in a school building was hindering our growth. Problems with the schedule aside, many of the people we were trying to reach strongly associated school with past failures. Although the free rent made the space attractive to us initially, the main reason we thought the location would work well was that it offered on-site job training for specific areas like cosmetology, cooking, and computers. However, once we started working with job seekers, it became obvious that specific training was beyond the scope of what the majority needed from us. Our members required help with much more elementary problems like how to properly fill out a job application, write a resume, and conduct oneself in an interview.

Dave found us a new space a few miles away in a 10-story office building on West Seventh Street in the core of downtown. Over the Christmas holiday Beth personally oversaw our move into our new office. Ten men from one of our partner agencies, a local halfway house, came to work off some community service hours. By the second day they were whining and moaning about the cold. An armed probation officer was overseeing them. Suddenly one of them ran. "Here, you watch them," said the officer as he started pursuing the runner.

Just six weeks after her surgery, Beth was faced with the task of keeping the rest of the men from following their buddy's example. Calmly Beth asked them to all sit down.

"I hate to move as much as the next person," said Beth, who maintained her sense of humor. "But it's your choice: five years in jail, or two more weeks of community service."

Luckily, they stayed seated on the sidewalk.

CHAPTER 5

If You Build It, They Will Come—Won't They?

"I knew there was a way out. I knew there was another kind of life because I had read about it. I knew there were other places, and there was another way of being."
–Oprah Winfrey

Once we moved to the new location in the heart of downtown, we were encouraged by an immediate uptick in the number of job seekers coming in. Most could reach our new space with a single bus ride. In addition to improved accessibility, the move gave us much-needed space and visibility. We'd also eliminated a major hindrance in that several job seekers had felt uncomfortable in a school setting, which was for many a painful reminder of past failures.

From our viewpoint, the most important advantage that our new office delivered was that we were no longer shackled by the school schedule. Now we were able to mimic the hours and work schedules of the corporate world.

We conducted business from 8 a.m. to 4:30 p.m. Monday through Friday. The doors opened at 7:30 a.m. to early arrivals anxious about being on time. We only closed our doors on major holidays, and we ran workshops every week, with the exception of the week of Thanksgiving and the week between

Christmas and the New Year. Poverty doesn't take a holiday, and we wanted the poor we were serving to know they could count on us.

Adding to Beth's challenging health situation, she mysteriously lost her voice midway through that year. Ultimately she was diagnosed with vocal cord paralysis. For the next year she spoke in a whisper and sounded like she constantly had laryngitis. Unfazed, she found a portable microphone to use at meetings and in the workshop.

Newspaper articles proved to be a mixed blessing. Some described our services accurately and told our story well. Other reporters failed to take the time to learn what we were all about and put a negative spin on our story.

"How can you find anything negative to say about a program that is privately funded, founded by two dollar-a-year volunteers, and helps poor people acquire and retain jobs?" I fumed when an article appeared insinuating that we were somehow benefiting financially when in fact we had invested a substantial amount of our own money in the project.

Dave shared my irritation but replied, "We've just got to learn who writes fair stories and steer clear of the rest of them."

Because I didn't see a connection between news articles and an increase in job seekers, we chose not to spend our time and resources seeking any sort of publicity. Besides, we were too busy figuring out the model.

The new millennium ushered in a host of changes. First we changed our screening process for identifying appropriate candidates—again. At first we did it one-on-one. As demand for our services increased, this became too time-consuming, and we adopted a group approach, which did not work well because it was restricted to a few times a week. Next we tried the one-on-one approach again, but quickly abandoned it once again as it simply took too much time.

In our new space we started holding an orientation for groups four mornings a week. At that time, potential members were introduced to the Cincinnati Works program. Our recruiter Nancy explained that our goal was to help our members move from poverty to self-sufficiency by helping them get a permanent, full-time position that provides health benefits.

"We are not just another job training program," she said. "During our mandatory job readiness workshop, we'll help you learn the skills you need to get and retain a job, skills like resume preparation, time management, and the hidden rules of the work world."

She also laid out the ground rules of our job readiness workshop, which we had whittled down to an intensive single week by that point.

"You must be in the classroom by 9 a.m. sharp or the door will be locked," she continued. "You must attend every class. If you have an emergency, you will be allowed to make up the class or classes you missed during the next two weeks. However, if you do not complete all the classes in that timeframe, you will have to start the workshop over again in order to become a Cincinnati Works member."

Early on we gave more latitude, but we found that more and more of our workshop attendees had excuses to miss segments of the workshop, many of which seemed legitimate. Although we offered a warm, supportive atmosphere, we realized that these "emergencies" were products of the same behaviors that cost the potential members jobs in the first place. Subsequently we installed standards for workshop attendance that mirrored the real work world.

Those who were still interested after the group orientation filled out an application and stayed for an interview with the recruiter to determine their eligibility. We accepted adults age 18 and older who could pass a drug screen and who did not have a violent criminal record or one that was repetitive in nature. We used to drug screen when we did the introduction, but due to the no-show rate for the workshop, we found we saved a lot of money by waiting until the first day of the workshop.

We also required that applicants have a stable residence. That requirement enabled them to concentrate on the modules and allowed potential employers to reach them more easily. Someone in a drug or alcohol rehabilitation program was typically not ready for the additional commitment of working, because of the danger of relapse.

We let applicants know that they should not start the workshop on a week when they had scheduled any other appointments. Originally we thought a general educational development (GED) diploma would be a minimum requirement, but we found some employers who would hire candidates without one.

Today we hold orientation two days a week. It's also possible for job seekers to come to our office at other times, fill out an application, talk to the recruiter, and find out if they are eligible for our program.

After three years in operation we still struggled with recruiting. The numbers of men coming through our doors had slowly climbed from the 10% we had when we began tracking numbers. However, we still couldn't understand why more poor people—particularly men—weren't coming to us for help. More than 175,000 people were living in poverty in our region, and more than 10,000 entry-level jobs that fit the Cincinnati Works criteria were still going unfilled each year.

Where was the disconnect? Some adults did not qualify for our program because of violent police records, drug and alcohol addictions, or serious mental health issues that were beyond our capacity to help. But by our estimates that left more than 70,000 adults living in poverty in the Greater Cincinnati region whom we could help.

Where were they? Why didn't they come streaming through our doors? What were we missing? These questions filled our minds. At times Dave and I wondered if we had made a grave mistake. Had we accepted funding from friends and acquaintances for something we couldn't deliver?

In December 1998, we once again turned to Steven Howe, Ph.D., a University of Cincinnati psychology professor, for answers. We didn't have computers when we launched the program in 1996, but in 1997 we built a computer database with detailed records. The professor carefully sifted through our records to sort out who was most likely to show up for the first day of the workshop. Shortly before we moved our offices, he delivered the results of the study on members and their job searches.

His research turned up some answers that we expected, but it also raised some issues that were a surprise. His analysis showed which candidates were most likely to follow through after the initial interview and actually attend the workshop. They included:

- People who were currently working part-time or who had worked within the last two years

- People who had children age 18 or younger in their care and who were currently receiving public assistance
- Those who had a driver's license
- Those who had a nonviolent criminal record
- Those with current legal problems
- Those who expressed a need for help with job seeking skills; for example, interviewing skills, resume assistance, and job leads

We were stunned to discover that people with criminal records and legal problems were more likely to follow through. At first that fact seemed counterintuitive. But as we mulled it over, we attributed it to more accountability demanded from probation officers and to a strong desire to have support from an organization that could help them sort out their problems.

Dave and I weren't surprised when the numbers showed that men were less likely to show up for the first day of the workshop. Children in the home served as a powerful motivator, and so single moms were good candidates for the workshop. Our experience had shown that if a candidate didn't come for that first day, we were unlikely ever to see that person again.

The study provided us with some helpful clues as we redoubled our efforts at recruiting prospective members. Frustrated and determined, we still faced an arduous, uphill battle.

Recruitment affected every part of our business. If we couldn't recruit enough people, we wouldn't have sufficient numbers for the job readiness workshop, and we wouldn't produce enough graduates who got jobs and stayed at work.

A baffling phenomenon continued: Our no-show rate for the job readiness workshop hovered at about 50%. If 50 people were approved to start a readiness workshop, 25 showed up to start on Monday. If 10 people were approved to start, five showed up.

We struggled to understand why someone would bother to fill out an application, agree to submit to a police background check and a drug screen, and then not follow through by coming to the workshop.

We suspected that when some candidates got a more thorough understanding of what we were all about—that we didn't give people jobs or do specific job training but rather assisted them in getting their own jobs—they lost interest. They were living in survival mode and had difficulty comprehending that an investment of time for long-term gain was wise when they saw their need as so immediate. We could only surmise that they were so used to complying with authority that they filled out the application anyway and failed to indicate that they were no longer interested.

Drugs were—and still are—likely the biggest reason people failed to show up for the workshop. We screen all workshop attendees for drugs because employers in Ohio receive a reduction in their worker's compensation if they maintain a drug-free workplace. Since potential job seekers are told up front that we screen for drugs before allowing anyone into the program, they take themselves out of the process if they know they can't pass.

Recently we tweaked our policy because we were losing so many people who tested positive for marijuana. Now everyone accepted into our program can go through the workshop without a drug screen. During the workshop, the participants are able to connect with staff and learn about the advantages of healthy living. The drug test is administered on Friday, the fifth day of the workshop. If a test is positive for marijuana, that person is allowed to job search, but not with our core employers. Only people who pass the drug screen are able to get employment with a company that pays higher wages, has benefits, and offers possibility for advancement. The reasoning behind this change is that job seekers have a chance to interact with an encouraging staff and work with a mental health counselor who is able to assist many job seekers in giving up marijuana.

The draw of the underground economy is a significant reason potential clients don't follow through with the workshop. We don't know the full extent to which it plays a role in the lives of our members, but we do know what people have shared with us. There is the strong temptation of the illicit drug trade, under-the-table day jobs where income is not reported, and even a bartering system through which people exchange goods and services. Many people live with relatives or friends and keep moving as needed. The underground economy not only keeps people in poverty from coming to Cincinnati Works, it also enables some to be selective about the jobs they are willing to do.

Far from being discouraged by the study's results and the slow progress we were making, we redoubled our efforts. We made presentations to various agencies like Hamilton County Jobs and Family Services and Freestore Foodbank to let them know about our services and to put referral procedures in place. However, we found that many people who were referred by the Department of Jobs and Family Services and other agencies were often less serious about going to work. Often they complied simply to fulfill the county's requirements for continuing public assistance.

Within a year of our startup, we started running ads in *Employment Guide* (now called *Job List*), a weekly newspaper that featured job leads. That became our best recruitment tool by the time we moved to the new office, producing half of all our candidates. It remains one of our top sources today. It was free, readily available on the street, and it was focused on what the poor cared about, which was finding jobs. Most importantly, people who were reading *Employment Guide* were generally more motivated and were actively looking for employment.

Once we moved to our new location, referrals from participants who had become members gradually emerged as another big source of new candidates. Word-of-mouth referrals pleased us the most because they let us know we had a satisfied customer. We started giving incentives in the form of gift certificates through our partnership with Kroger, a grocery store chain, and Frisch's Big Boy, a Midwestern chain of casual family restaurants. Soon referrals from friends and family who had become Cincinnati Works members accounted for more than 50% of our job seekers.

One segment of our targeted population particularly puzzled us. The Appalachian community makes up 60% of those in poverty in our region, but they represented a much smaller proportion of our workshop attendees. We tried to develop relationships within the community by connecting with some of their leaders and conducting workshops in their communities. But none of our efforts garnered much response. Those who did come were less interested in getting a job than in having a place to socialize. We had hoped that our new location would be more attractive to the Appalachian poor, but the numbers remained low.

Undaunted, we met with experts on this culture from the
College of Mount St. Joseph. They confirmed our experiences
with the poor from those communities. Many Appalachians
share the following characteristics:

- Shy away from bureaucracy/government
- Feel threatened outside of their neighborhood
- Do not like change
- Are highly mobile (make many trips back home to
  Appalachia)
- Do not value education (high dropout rate)
- Want women to stay home and take care of the family
- High incidence of domestic abuse
- High rate of illiteracy
- Distrust childcare providers
- Have no desire for changes in their lifestyles
- Are deemed outcasts if they try to better themselves
- Support themselves with day labor, temporary jobs,
  or by selling items at craft and flea markets

We compared our numbers with the new census information.
In order to improve our recruitment efforts, we commissioned
Linda A. LaCharity, Ph.D., R.N., an assistant professor at the
University of Cincinnati's College of Nursing, to do a study
on our members' journeys toward self-sufficiency. The Health
Foundation of Greater Cincinnati underwrote the funding for
the study.

Dr. LaCharity explored and compared the characteristics of
45 of our members who fell into three categories: Group 1 was
composed of those who had retained employment for at least
a year; Group 2 was composed of those who cycled in and out
of full-time employment, making frequent job changes, but

continued to seek our help in finding permanent employment; and Group 3 was made up of those who were ineffective at holding down a job or resistant to seeking employment.

Factors that were found to contribute to the desire to change and become self-sufficient were wanting to be independent and able to take care of family needs and responsibilities; wanting to provide a stable home environment; wanting to improve self-esteem; and wanting to be a good example for one's children. Several people mentioned that, since becoming Cincinnati Works members, they had been able to do such things as find their own apartments, purchase cars, buy new clothes for their children, pay bills on time, and start savings accounts.

"It's kind of exciting," one participant explained. "My babies see me doing something positive. And we have a TV now 'cause Momma's working, and the phone's turned on. I can take care of things for my kids, and for the first time in my life, I have a savings account. It's not much, but it's ours." Twenty-five of the participants specifically mentioned a desire to further their educations.

"I didn't want my children to have to struggle like I did," said one participant.

Another added, "I had to go back and get some education to get a job I'd like doing. Just bouncing from job to job is not good for you."

Providing for the family proved a powerful motivator. One member said to the researcher, "I tell you, what really got my attention was one day my son came in the door from school, and school was 15 minutes walking distance away. And he came in that afternoon and said, 'Momma, I am so cold, you know this jacket just ain't warm enough.' And that made me feel really bad. I got my behind up and moving and I haven't sat down yet. I seen to it that I'll never hear anything like that again."

Several members expressed the emotional longing for the boost in self-esteem that comes with self-sufficiency. "The thing that motivated me was the need to feel that I'm doing my part, pulling my own load. It was mainly for my own self-esteem," said one member.

The most successful participants cited more motivating factors. "I haven't asked anyone for anything in I don't know how long," said a member from Group 1. "Independence was a goal ... a nice apartment, a nice vehicle, nice everything. I have a good job. Those things make me feel rich. I'm not rich, but what I'm saying is that I feel rich."

Participants from the third group tended to name no more than one motivating factor for making a change and spoke of leaving life changes in the hands of God. Participants from the first two groups were more likely to be motivated by the potential to become independent and to be able to meet their financial obligations.

Most participants reported that their decision to make a life change was supported by family and friends. One commented, "They were in my corner and giving me praise. They were happy I was doing something to find a job."

In fact, 38 members responded that they felt their family and friends treated them with more respect now that they were employed. "I noticed a difference when I went to the store," said one member. "Before I would use food stamps and vouchers, and I always tried to hide it. Now I feel better being able to use cash. And you know, if someone ahead of me in line is using the stamps, I make sure not to give them a terrible look. That was me a few years ago."

Surprisingly, pay wasn't listed as the most important factor about a job. Participants were most concerned about benefits (health, dental, and life insurance, as well as savings plans), the type of work, good coworkers, and a challenge. Several described their ideal job as one they could look forward to every day. "What I want is a job I can look forward to ... A job that, maybe, if I think about it off the job, it's a pleasant thought," one member shared with us.

The two most popular forms of employment were business-oriented work and healthcare. In terms of business, members generally sought jobs as entry-level receptionists, cashiers, and clerks, but some landed positions ranging from accounting to marketing to owning their own businesses.

The third most popular kind of work was that which required manual labor—construction, manufacturing, and housekeeping. Some participants mentioned electronics repair, childcare, and beautician/barber care. A few participants dreamed of work in creative fields, such as drawing, cartooning, or playing music.

When not working at a steady job, the members who participated in the study managed to get by using a variety of tactics: 27 members (60%) relied on public assistance; 18 (40%) picked up odd jobs and did temporary work through agencies; 13 (29%) accepted public assistance and help from family and friends; eight (18%) were completely supported by others; and eight (18%) admitted to illegal activities. Some members did odd jobs like running errands for elderly neighbors, helping people move, and delivering phone books. Those in groups 2 and 3 were twice as likely to get work through temporary agencies as were those in group 1. One member described the discouraging cycle of working with these agencies: "The ones I been going to are mainly temporary agencies. They work me for like two or three weeks, and then I'm back on the corner again where I was before. It makes you feel kind of fed up and discouraged."

Some survived by getting favors from friends: loans, a temporary place to stay, babysitting services, bags of groceries, and offers of transportation. Some bartered services like taking care of physically disabled adults or children. Illegal activities ran the gamut from selling drugs to offering unlicensed beautician services. Some members relied heavily on knowing where to get services in the community: the Free Store, free health clinics, the Salvation Army, various thrift stores, and the emergency services provided by the county government.

Seeing where wrong choices led was enough to motivate some of the participants. One member offered: "I seen a lot of my friends, and they were going the wrong way, getting into trouble and going to jail, and I didn't want that to be me, so I basically made up my mind to change right there and then."

Some members considered their family members hindrances—especially ex-spouses and parents. "I was moving away. I was moving up, and I guess my parents were afraid of losing contact with me or seeing me progress," said a participant.

We were constantly striving to learn more about what barriers to steady employment our members were contending with. Those in Group 3 perceived almost four times the number of barriers mentioned by those in Group 1. Participants in Group 1 most commonly cited transportation and fear of rejection as barriers, while those in Group 3 more frequently cited lack of education, poor work history, and self-esteem issues in addition to transportation.

Almost half of the participants in this study said that their fear of failure or rejection presented a barrier. "It's very frightening looking for a job," said one. "Being rejected makes me feel disappointed in myself," confided another. "I wonder how and where did I go wrong." Some members described the deep anxiety they felt after submitting a resume or going for an interview and then not getting any feedback. For some the fear became immobilizing. "Just the fear of leaving the house, going out and getting the job, the fear of being turned down or being pushed away, the fear that they won't call you back or that you might get bad news," one member said.

All of the members surveyed who had been formally diagnosed with depression fell into Group 3. Many described drug and alcohol abuse stemming from physical or mental abuse growing up. One eloquently described how having a job helped lift the fog of depression: "I think not having a job magnifies my depression, with isolation … the sense of wrongness. But when I'm working and I'm in my little rut jobwise, I feel great. I have a purpose. I have a sense of being okay. I feel like I belong, like I'm connected."

These participants required therapy before they could tackle the job market.

More than a third (16) mentioned poor self-esteem, while 18 noted lack of support. Twelve cited abuse (both as an adult and as a child), but hardly any of the participants were comfortable offering any details on this topic.

While 38 of the 45 members the nurse surveyed admitted using substances, only 16 said they had a history of substance abuse. Most commonly people reported using alcohol, and some used marijuana.

One participant mentioned what she called the "generational curse" as a barrier. She expressed dismay at seeing children who grew up in poverty following in their parents' footsteps and struggling with substance abuse, physical/mental abuse, and reliance on welfare. Nineteen others in the group shared her concern. One said, "I guess it flows back to the role models. If you grow up around a bunch of people who aren't working, then that's the thing you grow up to do. I guess you start thinking that's how you're supposed to live your life."

One of the surprises that came out of this study was that 24 of the 45 respondents—though almost none of them had been professionally diagnosed—considered a perceived learning disability to be a stumbling block along the journey to self-sufficiency. Members of Group 2 and Group 3 spoke of their weaknesses in reading and math skills, with members of Group 3 being twice as likely as those from Group 2 to identify these barriers.

"My handwriting is bad, and I can't spell well. I couldn't even read those forms you gave me. I just kind of skimmed it," said one.

Another expressed frustration over not being able to "read the baseball scores on TV or any kind of stats they flash up."

Five members said their children's learning disabilities required extra time and attention that created a barrier.

Across all three groups health issues—their own and their children's—cropped up as a key barrier affecting the member's ability to retain a job, which convinced us more than ever that helping our members find jobs that offered health benefits was critical to their long-term success. Group 2 participants were twice as likely to have physical health problems. Several from this group described suffering from an injury or physical challenge that kept them from doing the type of work they had previously done. Their desire to work was tempered by their concern over aggravating their health problems, which ranged from back injuries to asthma.

A lack of stable housing was also frequently mentioned as a barrier. Our members were generally not homeowners, and the lack of steady employment prevented many from being able to pay rent and utilities regularly. Job seekers who cited a desire to provide for their families as motivation to use the support Cincinnati Works provided often discussed their desire to maintain a steady place of residence.

When asked which barrier was most difficult to overcome while attempting to make the transition to self-sufficiency, the overwhelming majority of respondents focused on issues related directly to the job search and the steps necessary to successfully obtain a job. Those first steps were often the hardest, and we were happy to confirm that, by walking our members through these steps, we were partnering with them to conquer some of their biggest obstacles. Just the simple act of getting out of bed and going to an interview was difficult for many, along with overcoming their fear of rejection.

We were supplying exactly the kind of help our members needed. All participants said that they would recommend our program to others. Even more encouraging, 39 made that statement with no prompting. Participants stressed spiritual faith, belief in oneself, and the need to remain focused as ways to achieve goals.

We were on the right track. We just needed to keep the faith.

CHAPTER 6

Figuring Out the Puzzle

"The poor themselves can create a poverty-free world ... all we have to do is to free them from the chains that we have put around them."

—Muhammad Yunus

Our move to the new offices coincided with an important milestone in any organization—the fourth anniversary of our opening. After four years in operation, we had learned a lot. With our understanding of the poor we served on a daily basis growing, we decided to increase the services we offered on-site. With more space, we now had the luxury to do that.

One of the biggest challenges people in poverty battle to this day is that the services that give them much-needed support usually require them to visit several different agencies or providers. Ask almost any person in poverty what one of the main barriers keeping them from getting a good job is, and transportation is likely to be named. Yet the system requires that people who need assistance waste precious energy, time, and money going from place to place to appear in person in order to get it. We reasoned that the more barrier-busting support we could provide in a single location, the more we could improve our members' chances of success.

Although the core of our services—providing such job seeking skills as how to fill out an application, how to present yourself during an interview, and how to dress on the job, and then providing follow-up with life skills coaching once our members got jobs—remained the same, we decided to see if we could improve the success of our members by offering more services on-site.

By this point in our growth, we had developed a snapshot of the people we were serving:

- 31% didn't have a high school diploma or GED
- 42% had a criminal record
- 60% suffered from depression or anxiety
- 60% had a poor work history
- 60% had graduated high school or had attended college
- 84% were African American; 14% were white; 2% represented other races
- The average age was 33
- 70% were women; 30% were men
- 40% had children who were minors

Two issues stood out overwhelmingly, one of which we'd already begun to address on-site. Members in all three groups that Linda LaCharity identified reported dealing with a tremendous number of struggles related to mental health—depression, abuse, poor self-esteem, behavioral and emotional problems, family issues, substance abuse, anxiety, and fear of rejection based on so many past failures. Too often, the fear of failure and low self-esteem conspired to paralyze them.

Based on LaCharity's research, building spiritual resources emerged as the next area after mental health where we thought our members could significantly benefit from on-site support.

To the questions "What thing in your life has helped you the most?" and "What have you been missing?" our members across the board gave answers that had a spiritual component. Dave and I discussed how to address that need while Beth took on the search for a new on-site counselor. Our vision was that the ideal candidate would function somewhat like a hospital chaplain—not pushing any specific religious agenda, but offering comfort and a listening ear.

We found Sister Jeanne Marie, a retired nun with the Sisters of Notre Dame, in 2000. A short, spunky woman in her late 60s with a kind smile, she had been doing home repairs for seniors, but she was looking for a new challenge.

We were a little concerned at first that some members might shy away from meeting with a nun, but most quickly warmed to Sister Jeanne, who left her short, salt and pepper hair uncovered and didn't wear a formal habit.

We converted an old stairwell into a small office where she could meet privately with members. She took over teaching the module on values and ethics, which introduced her to the workshop attendees on neutral territory. On Friday afternoons she met with job seekers one-on-one to get their impressions of the workshop and help them process what they'd learned from the week.

"The members like me because I'm the only one who doesn't ask them to do something," laughed Sister Jeanne. Mostly she offered encouragement and her skills as a listener. Coming from a solid family life, Sister Jeanne was amazed to learn how many barriers people faced. "The poor don't have role models; they don't have confidence. They don't believe in themselves," she said. "They don't have a base."

Sister Jeanne noted that about 20% of those in the workshop suffered from some degree of illiteracy. They learned to compensate, cover up, and make excuses to hide their lack of abilities.

"People who are poor are pushed around," she said. "They are used to showing up and having to wait and wait and wait. Nobody honors appointments. When I meet with our members, I'm careful to honor the time and to be available. They have dealt with so much frustration and disappointment in their lives, I want my office to be a refuge for them."

Gradually Sister Jeanne noticed that men were more likely to seek her out. "They show me photos of their kids," she said. "A lot of them have been brought up by their grandmothers or by single moms, so they gravitate toward women. The members want to connect and are looking for affirmation."

When members graduated from the workshop, Sister Jeanne called them once a month for the first three months. "Very few call back, but I just want them to hear a friendly voice and to know I'm thinking about them," she said cheerily.

Members often dropped by her small, tidy office, which she nicknamed The Well, and nervously asked her to pray with them before they headed to a job interview. When they thought their interviews had gone well, they often popped their heads into her spartan space, which had a few inspirational posters on the wall and a small tabletop fountain gurgling, and shared the good news.

As for the mental health side of the equation, Beth began searching for a better fit to serve our members on-site, someone who would concentrate on assisting members for the purpose of enabling them to get and keep a job.

In December 2000 she found Jacque Edmerson, who had a master's degree in social work and specialized in community mental health. Jacque had worked for 10 years in a mental health clinic that served the severely mentally ill in Hamilton County, where she had rapidly progressed to become the clinical director. Jacque resigned from that post after growing discouraged and depressed about changes the government made that she thought were taking services for the severely mentally ill in the wrong direction.

She launched a small consulting business that worked with a welfare-to-work program, and she did part-time work for a temporary agency that specialized in placing mental health professionals. Because she had become so disenchanted with social work, she was actually reluctant to interview for the position with Cincinnati Works. The third oldest of seven children who grew up in a poor neighborhood—Cincinnati's West End—and the first in her immediate family to graduate from college, Jacque brought an understanding of the need to stabilize people as quickly as possible in order to get them working. She understood that she wouldn't have time to delve into years and years of personal history with each member.

In the mental health related segments of the workshop Jacque taught—such as attitudes and conflict management—she quickly became popular with the job seekers. A petite, snappy dresser with a warm smile, she deftly blended streetwise pronouncements and her own life experiences with solid behavioral science to help workshop attendees get a better understanding of themselves and the unfamiliar world of work. They came to think of Jacque as just part of the staff and got to know her on neutral territory.

As our mental health counselor, Jacque worked hard to build trust with those she tried to help before she could get to the real issues that were holding the job seekers back. Because her office was on-site, and because all job seekers were required to check in with her, they didn't feel singled out or intimidated. She helped job seekers to see conflict as an opportunity to exercise problem solving skills.

"I really believe God put me here so that I could use what I've learned in my own life to help change other people's lives," Jacque said.

On a good day somebody with depression and anxiety can get a job, but then a bad day comes and they can't keep the job. Unfortunately, when the middle class encounters a person in poverty suffering from depression or anxiety, they tend to label that person lazy. They think, "Why don't they just get a job?"

The street teaches our job seekers to self-medicate with drugs and alcohol in order to feel better, but that usually just makes the depression worse. Others numb themselves by avoiding having to deal with problems. Many of our members have not learned basic problem solving.

Jacque understood this population. During the workshop and in private sessions, she helped our members devise plans to get specific skills training in order to manage their lives differently and break the cycle of living in crisis. She did what was necessary to stabilize people in the workplace. The act of working itself helped people begin to feel better about themselves. Trying to solve all of their problems before they ever started working wasn't real-world thinking. Our goal was for them to go to work for companies that included mental health care in their health insurance policies so they qualified for long-term mental health benefits.

A young, pretty woman sat in Jacque's office crying her eyes out.

"That will guarantee you won't be successful," Jacque told the woman firmly when she blurted out her intention to quit her new job because of scheduling conflicts with her children's school. "You can do it. You've made some bad choices, but you can make this work. Call the board of education. You have four children to think about. It can't be about you at this point."

The young woman left home at age 15 because of constant fights with her mother, an addict. "Every time you start to get your life together, you make bad choices because you think you don't deserve anything. I'm asking you to prove to yourself and others that you do."

Jacque understood that this member was caught in a cycle of living in crisis. Her lack of problem solving skills, combined with depression, inhibited her ability to make good choices. Drying her tears, the member promised Jacque that she'd stick with her job. Then suddenly she jumped up. "I just remembered I'm double parked," she said, racing for the elevator.

Jacque shook her head and sighed deeply. "Most of us would look at her situation and her need to support four children and think, 'How in the world could you even think about quitting your job?' And yet our members do quit, because they function in that constant state of crisis," she said to me. "I sure hope she didn't get towed."

Many of our members get caught in the undertow of some crisis or another. Before long one problem has snowballed and become an avalanche of trouble that takes them down. Ruth, a single mom with four kids, came to us in full-blown crisis mode. After being injured in a car accident and taking time off to care for her mother who was dying of cancer, Ruth lost her job as a clerk at a ball bearing company. Next her car was repossessed. Then she and her children were left homeless after being evicted from their apartment.

After several months of staying with friends and in motels, Ruth called a homeless shelter. By that point she had been unemployed going on two years, and her self-esteem was almost nonexistent. "Who would want to hire me with little kids?" wondered the high school graduate. "I felt so stupid."

A caseworker told her about Cincinnati Works. After completing the workshop and getting counseling from Jacque, Ruth landed a job in customer service with Fifth Third Bank. Her employment support specialist followed up with her weekly, then monthly, then quarterly to make sure she was on track. Within months she was promoted to the position of loan closer.

Ben, 48 years old and married for 13 years with no children, came to us with a history of low-functioning skills in school, though he had learned to read. When his employment support specialist referred him to Jacque, he claimed to have had more than 50 jobs. He lost three temp-to-hire jobs during his first six months in counseling. Our counselor recognized that he needed additional services, so she referred him to the mental health system for psychiatric assessment; he was diagnosed with depression and went on medication.

Ben was then referred to the Ohio Bureau of Vocational Rehabilitation for assessment of skill level, skill enhancement, and a job coach. That agency worked with him on building self-esteem, self-confidence, setting boundaries, negative/self-defeating thinking issues, and fear. He did not work for a year while undertaking this development program. After one year, he got a job in a factory and held it for 18 months, the longest he had worked at any place in 10 years. But he lost that job, a 45-minute drive from his home, due to an issue common among our members: His car broke down.

At that point he reconnected with Cincinnati Works. He found another job but was not happy with his $8.24 hourly pay. He continued to meet with Jacque to stay focused on realistic expectations of his employer, keep an upbeat/positive attitude, and to continue to hone his general problem solving skills. He needed ongoing support and encouragement. Most of the folks our counselor saw did not need this level of help, nor were many willing to work the process as hard as Ben did.

The gratitude our members offered the staff boosted our determination to keep pushing forward. They often penned thank you notes to different staff members who had touched their lives in some way. We started pinning the thank you notes on what we dubbed "The Wall of Gratitude" in our lobby. It encouraged the staff and gave newcomers an idea of the sort of warmth and support they would experience if they completed our program.

Soon after we moved to our new building, Anthony Carson dropped by to see Beth. He had gotten a promotion at his job at the hotel just around the corner. He also knew she was undergoing chemo and wanted to see how she was doing.

"How would you like to work here in the afternoons cleaning up?" Beth asked.

Anthony jumped at the chance to add a few hours' wages to his income. He worked the 11:30 p.m. to 7:30 a.m. shift at the hotel, then he would head home to sleep, and he came in to clean our offices around 3 p.m.

"That was in 2000, around the time Beth was being treated for breast cancer, and I've been here ever since," recalled Anthony. "I wanted to stay close to the organization. I was excited about Cincinnati Works because it helps black folks. I know it's for everyone, but in my class, there were 17 of us and only one white person. It struck me because few organizations out there beyond temp services help black people find work. A lot of organizations say they want to help us, but I don't see the action.

"It's not hard to see what's going on in our community. That's why I'm so hard on my son. These boys want to wear their pants down below their butts and act the fool. Peer pressure is a monster for these kids. We need people like the folks at Cincinnati Works who genuinely care about us and our children."

For Anthony, born in West End and raised in Winton Terrace, one of six major public housing projects in Cincinnati, the road out of the projects was a bumpy one. When he was just five years old, his father, a baker who worked in the galley on the *Delta Queen,* left Anthony, his two sisters, his brother, and his mom and went to New York City. Later Anthony learned that his mother had thrown his father out, tired of the drama caused by his hard drinking and carousing.

"I loved my father, but he had to go," said Anthony. "He was into some real bad things, and my mother just didn't want those things around us."

When Anthony turned 13, his mother, who worked steadily at Kenner Products for more than three decades, sent him to live with his grandmother upon his grandfather's death. His grandmother handled bets on sporting events in the neighborhood and cooked barbeque, selling it out of her kitchen. When Anthony was 16, he saw his father for what turned out to be the last time.

"I dreamed of being a baseball player or an actor," said Anthony. "But I got on the wrong track—chasing girls, drinking, smoking pot."

He dropped out of a performing arts high school in the 11th grade at age 18. Soon the young man who barely knew his own father learned from his high school girlfriend that he was going to become a father himself. He turned down an offer from a semi-pro baseball team because he knew the money wouldn't be enough to support a baby.

"When my daughter, Michele, was born, I wanted to be there for her," he said. "I didn't want to be like my dad. I decided a long time ago that if I ever had a family, I was going to take care of them."

Anthony's mom, by that time a supervisor at Kenner, which made dolls like Strawberry Shortcake and popular action figures from movies like *Star Wars* and *Indiana Jones,* helped him get a job in Kenner's maintenance department. He also briefly held a job with the City of Cincinnati Recreation Department.

He paid child support for his daughter but steered clear of other relationships.

"When my father left, I said if I ever got married I'd be there for my family and my wife," he explained. "I was a bachelor for 10 years because I figured if I can't take care of me, I sure can't take care of a family."

Then Anthony met Angela, who was from Dayton. After 18 months of dating, he asked her to move in with him. "Angela said, 'I'll live with you if you marry me,'" he said, "so we got married. My queen, my wife was the biggest change in my life. I give her and the Lord more credit than anyone."

Daughter Arielle came a year after they married, followed by Anthony Jr. With their savings the couple bought a nice house on one of the tree-lined streets of College Hill, a diverse and vibrant community on the northwest edge of downtown Cincinnati.

Anthony is proud that he was able to break the chain of generational poverty and has fought hard to create a better life for his kids.

"Without the Lord behind you, you're going nowhere," Anthony said. "I'm saved. I've been dipped in the water. I ain't where I should be, but I got saved after I lost my job in 1996. The Lord will work on you until you get where you need to be. You gotta want to be somebody and make a difference in this world. I didn't just want to be a wine-head on a corner or a guy lying up under a bridge sleeping in my old neighborhood. I could have been him, but the Lord has blessed me with good people in my life."

Every day at Cincinnati Works brought surprises. One single mom got the bald tires on her car replaced, thanks to a fund established by our board member Kent Friel and his wife to help remove unusual barriers our members faced. She came in shortly before Christmas that year, after several months on her new job, and proudly presented Beth with an envelope.

"Here," she said, grinning broadly. "This is the money you loaned me for the tires. Now you can use it for somebody else."

When Beth opened the envelope, she found 100 neatly ordered singles. Our president broke down in tears.

CHAPTER 7

Job Readiness Workshop: Lock the Door

"A gem cannot be polished without friction,
nor a man perfected without trials."
–Lucius Annaeus Seneca

It was Monday, 9 a.m. sharp, and 11 people—a diverse group composed of seven women and four men—were seated around three round tables. Their names were on cards in front of their seats. The cards at two places bore the names of job seekers who hadn't arrived yet, which meant they had already broken the first rule of the program: We demand punctuality. Employers expect it, and so we do too. Those who were present looked somewhat anxious, and the room was quiet.

When Frank, the welcome session's facilitator, strode confidently into the room, he closed the door firmly behind him and locked it. Dressed professionally, he exuded a warm yet no-nonsense attitude.

"Good morning, ladies and gentlemen," said Frank cheerily, flashing a smile. "Welcome."

He called out the attendees' names, acknowledging each with his gaze. He mentioned the two who were absent and optimistically speculated that perhaps they would make the afternoon session, even though past experience told us that the morning no-shows were unlikely to turn up at all.

Then Frank got straight down to business, explaining what the workshop covered and what was expected of the participants. He handed out applications to the job seekers and gave them their first assignment: Bring back the completed application and three references with full contact information by the next morning.

The purpose of Cincinnati Works' mandatory, week-long job readiness workshop was twofold: First, it was designed to teach the soft skills necessary for obtaining and keeping a job. This workshop provided the first bridge between the employer and the member and was used as a tool to share information with the job seeker. Almost all of the job seekers who came to us had held jobs in the past, but because they lacked the ability to manage anger, problem solve, and the like, most were unable to retain those jobs for any substantial length of time. Some came to the workshop with a know-it-all attitude, sure that they understood everything about the world of work. However, in exit interviews, virtually everyone who successfully completed the workshop acknowledged that they learned many tips that would make them more attractive as prospective employees and help them succeed in the long term.

The second purpose of the job readiness workshop, which was just as crucial as the first, was that during the course of the workshop the Cincinnati Works team gained valuable information about each individual's life situation, behavior, attitude, motivation, and commitment to the process. Observing the interactions of folks in a workshop setting helped our team identify potential problems on the jobsite so that we would know how to coach the Cincinnati Works members through challenges that inevitably arose when they entered the work world.

All job seekers were required to successfully complete all modules of the workshop before they were allowed to participate in a job search. Some potential job seekers told our recruiter in desperate tones, "I need a job, not a class." We gently suggested that they get a day labor job and return when they were able to dedicate the time needed. Sadly, many had been without a job for weeks or months, and yet they couldn't see the value of investing a week of their time in a workshop that would likely lead to job security and advancement.

Our team members trained classes ranging in size from 8 to 30 attendees. The age range was anywhere from 18 to 70+, although the average attendee was in his or her mid-30s. After we moved into our new offices, more and more men took the classes. The majority of our job seekers were still African American, but we did start seeing more diversity at the new location. What remained constant was the mind-boggling combination of barriers the attendees faced in their quests to find good jobs.

We vacillated about the length of the workshop and what our policy should be in regard to attendance. Though we started out with a three-week workshop, it did not take long for us to realize that some of the things we were teaching were not essential to getting and keeping a job. Besides, the three-week workshop requirement sounded like an eternity to the people we were trying to help. Relatively few were willing to make that kind of commitment, we had trouble keeping potential members motivated to wait several weeks for the next workshop to begin, and the length and intensity of the workshop limited the number of people we could work with.

After a few months we eliminated some of the curriculum and went with a two-week workshop. Then, not long after we moved to our new building, we winnowed the curriculum to a one-week, 33-hour workshop arranged in modules that emphasized the basics our core employers stressed were important to them. We found that members learned the most about work by working. Therefore, the quicker people got to work, the sooner they were able to practice the new behaviors acquired during the workshop.

Since each week the curriculum of the workshop was exactly the same as all the other weeks, job seekers were able to make up a module the next week if they needed to miss one during their workshop. In the wake of this shift, our members became more successful at landing jobs, and their job retention rate held steady. Another bonus to shortening the workshop: We were able to accommodate three times the number of job seekers.

Like the workshop length, our attendance policy evolved over the years too. At first we allowed several absences for legitimate reasons. That did not work because too many of these "legitimate reasons" would not have been accepted by an employer as good enough to miss work. A no-exceptions policy better reflected the reality of the workplace and employers' expectations. The workshop facilitator and trainers were also happy to relinquish the role of enforcers. Instead, learning to follow rules became the focus.

Once the module structure was put in place, 100% attendance became a requirement. Even though we discouraged job seekers from starting the workshop if they had any appointments during the week, we acknowledged that unexpected things do come up. Our new policy allowed a job seeker to miss a module and then make it up in another workshop. It just delayed the person's entry into the job search. We required that the makeup module be completed within a two-week period. If it wasn't, the job seeker had to start over and repeat the entire workshop.

Not only were the job seekers expected to attend every module, they were expected to be in their seats on time. If they took a break, they had to be back at the designated time. When the workshop was shortened to one week, the lunch hour was reduced to 30 minutes. We encouraged attendees to bring their lunches because it was almost impossible to go out for lunch and return within the allotted time.

Everything about the workshop was designed to reflect workplace policies. For this reason we made no exceptions to the policy on attendance and timeliness. To ensure adherence we locked the training room door when it was time to start. Anyone left outside had to make up that module.

On Tuesday morning the first module was taught by Jacque, our mental health counselor, who covered the topics of attitudes and beliefs. Dressed in a crisp, white blouse, a black skirt, and heels, Jacque, who has achieved the highest level of education of anyone in her family, got right down to business: "This class covers attitudes and beliefs and how they affect us, both adversely and positively. You'll learn how you developed your attitudes and beliefs, how your family and your environment shapes your thinking. If you are going to change your life, you will have to change your thinking.

"When you think about work, how many of you have felt disappointed, maybe even angry?" she asked. Slowly, almost every hand in the room went up, and several heads nodded in acknowledgment. "Let's talk about the pain of feeling rejected and how that demonstrates itself in everyday life."

"Anger," said one young man at barely a whisper.

"Absolutely. Maybe your anger comes out verbally, or maybe you lash out at your coworkers or your boss. Maybe you're attitudinal when your employer asks you to do something. No matter the cause, anger turned inward feeds depression. Often, when you are depressed, you won't show up on time and your work performance is lackluster. Anger can easily lead you to sabotage yourself.

"Two weeks ago a 22-year-old woman with four children completed the same class you are in now. She moved out of her mother's house to find more stability. She found day care for her younger children and a good school for her oldest. But when I tell her how smart she is, she can't take the compliment—she doesn't see herself that way."

A nervous twitter of laughter erupted in one corner of the room. Jacque glanced at the neatly coiffed, heavyset woman, smiled at her, and continued. "I know how you think: 'I don't have nothing in place for my kids. Why am I going on this job interview anyway? Maybe I won't stick with the job. I probably won't even wake up on time.'

"So how do you start to change those negative thinking patterns? By age 18 your patterns of behavior are pretty well developed; they may be good … or not so good. Maybe you set goals, work to develop yourself, and strive to overcome the obstacles in your life. Or maybe you are one of those folks who has a problem with authority. You can't commit to anything, or you lie around and wait for things to happen for you."

She paused, scanning the room and gauging her audience's reaction. A few slumped at the tables, looking depressed; some appeared fearful and anxious, while others sat forward in their seats, listening intently.

"In order to change, we need to learn the steps to challenge our thinking. We can all talk about what we believe, but our actions and behaviors show our real core beliefs. You know you believe it if you practice it. *Practice being different.* "Live more consciously. Are you an impulsive person? Stop and think. Call before you quit. That 'pause button' is your opportunity to look at the ramifications of your decision. Process what you're thinking with us before you take action."

Then she asked the class to tell her some of the thoughts that ran through their minds when they thought about work, and she wrote them on the whiteboard at the front of the classroom:

- Everybody is out to get you.
- Supervisors think that you are beneath them.

The list grew longer. Then Jacque turned and said, "You can't be so motivated by others' actions. True power comes when you take responsibility for your actions and the consequences they bring. We'll talk more about how to resolve conflict in the session I teach on Thursday on conflict management."

Jacque counted teaching those modules as invaluable to her work with job seekers and members. "I begin to make observations about how they are with me and other members of the class," she said. "They get to know me as an individual, and by Friday when they have their required session with me, I'm just Jacque."

Likewise, teaching the modules enabled her to quickly connect with members individually. "Everything we do is on an individual basis," she said. "With 100 members, there will be 100 different approaches to giving them the support they need until they can make it on their own."

———— ∞∞∞ ————

On Wednesday morning the first module was titled
"Developing Quantified Selling Points" and was based on
material we adapted from WorkNet Publications. Everly Rose,
who was hired for advancement in 2001 and who taught this
session, entered the room with a big smile and asked, "Are
you getting hired today?"

Seated at two round tables were three men and five women.
One man and one woman from the previous day's workshop
were missing. A momentary shadow passed over Everly's
face as she noted their empty spots. "Maybe they'll join us
this afternoon," she said hopefully.

Next she passed out booklets. "I want you to write in these
books what you think are your good qualities," she instructed.
She gave them a few minutes and then asked, "Would anyone
be willing to share some of what you've written?"

"I worked security—responsibility and vigilant," one man
volunteered.

"I got laid off from a plant at Procter & Gamble. I worked
the assembly line," said an older woman. "Teamwork and
busy."

Everly interjected: "Draw on all experiences. Not just
work."

Another woman said, "I volunteered to register people for
Weight Watchers."

"Excellent," said Everly.

"Why do employers ask about your hobbies?" asked
someone else.

"Your hobbies may connect with the job," replied Everly.
"Hobbies can also help you connect with the interviewer. They

give the person clues as to who you are." She instructed the class to think through an example that demonstrated how they had used their strengths in the workplace or in life. "Never be without an answer, because employers will ask for an example," she said. "Don't weaken your interview by being caught without an answer."

Next she asked the workshop participants to list awards and memberships. "What is your greatest accomplishment?" she asked.

"Learning to drive."

"Graduating from high school."

A few more added similar answers.

"Good. Think of those as selling points," the facilitator said. "We are developing selling points for each of you. Those selling points are the key factors that are going to make an employer want to hire you."

Everly and the class worked through an exercise in which the job seekers list work experience and discuss how to deal with gaps in employment and periods during which one hopped from job to job. Again she emphasized the importance of preparing answers. "Maybe you were only on your last job for three months—be prepared to talk about having six years of work experience overall," she advised.

She used this discussion to emphasize why the concepts of "Call before you quit" (another idea adapted from WorkNet Publications) and "One job, one year" (an idea our legal advocate Jodie Ganote developed) were so vital to establishing workplace stability. "To be successful on the job, you need a good attitude, flexibility, perseverance, and strength." She wrote those four characteristics on the board under the word SUCCESS.

She described some of the ingredients of a good interview: "Smile and show enthusiasm and energy. Be open and flexible. Read the job description. Anticipate needs. What related information, education, seminars, and licenses do you have that will help you get that job? If you're interviewing for a job in customer service, for example, the interviewer might ask what angers you the quickest."

Right away the answers flew. "Rude people."

"When my boss talks down to me."

"When somebody disrespects me."

Everly smiled and said, "All honest answers, but if I'm interviewing you for a customer service position and I hear any of those answers, you're not going to get the job. Now, if you were to say something like, 'When my alarm clock doesn't go off,' you'd turn a potential negative into a positive, because you let the employer know you are concerned about being on time."

On the board she wrote:

Top 5 Reasons Employers Fire People
1. Poor attendance
2. Bad attitude
3. Tardiness
4. Poor performance
5. Dishonesty

The list provoked a lively discussion. Everly suggested that the job seekers write down their desired positions and then consider what positive qualities they had that someone hiring for that position would likely want.

A tall, gangly, 20-something man who said he wanted to be a food quality specialist rattled off his best qualities: "Flexible, knowledgeable, certified, good time management."

"Be sure to emphasize good time management, because that relates to three out of five of our 'Top 5 Reasons Employers Fire People,'" she advised. A former factory worker said she was "dependable, a team player, and good in a fast-paced environment." Everly continued helping the participants learn how to be specific about their good qualities.

Outside the classroom the cowbell rang twice, signifying that two different members had just landed jobs. The energy in the room shifted as everyone focused on the positives in their lives and heard confirmation that the hard work they were doing would likely be rewarded.

The instructor spent the remainder of the class helping the participants understand how important the accuracy of their job history was for employers and helping them learn how to discuss their individual barriers like terminations, job-hopping, and convictions.

One woman explained that she had lost her job as a bank teller a few months after the bank where she was employed was robbed. "After that I couldn't help but be jumpy with customers," she said.

The older woman who had formerly worked in a factory explained that she'd been in a head-on collision and had trouble keeping on task after that.

The instructor listened carefully and then said, "Don't give details on anything negative or emotional. Learn to say things like, 'I learned a valuable lesson. No longer will I let people or circumstances determine my behavior.' The lesson should be centered on you and what you've learned from your experiences."

Through the years our workshop facilitators have had to deal with many different kinds of situations. Successful facilitators are consistent but flexible, fair, compassionate, respectful, and maintain a sense of humor and an excellent work ethic. Most importantly, the facilitator, who teaches about half of the modules, must have a passion to assist people in becoming self-sufficient. If facilitators are not passionate about what they're doing, they will burn out quickly due to the energy it takes to give so much to groups with a lot of needs, week after week.

Many of our staff members were involved in presenting the workshop: Sister Jeanne taught a module called "Values and Building Confidence"; in addition to "Attitudes and Beliefs," our mental health counselor Jacque facilitated another session called "Conflict Resolution, Change, and Fear"; and our employment coordinator facilitated "The Employer Visit." The variety of presentations and viewpoints kept the workshop engaging. In the workplace job seekers would be dealing with a variety of personalities, so we designed the modules to reflect the real world and to incorporate skills and concepts our employer advisory committee told us employers need and expect. We worked hard to keep the message consistent even though the individual staff members' delivery styles were very different.

Workshop Schedule (Simplified)

MONDAY

- Professionalism
- Personality Inventory
- Skills Inventory
- Applications

TUESDAY

- Attitudes and Beliefs
- Networking

WEDNESDAY

- Interview Attire and Posture
- First 10 Seconds of an Interview
- 20-Second Commercial
- Think Like an Owner

THURSDAY

- Interview Idol
- Money and Budgeting

FRIDAY

- Conflict Resolution
- Change and Fear
- Mock Interviews
- Wellness and Health
- Goal Setting
- Graduation

Success Log ◆ Building Blocks ◆ Coretta Williams (Member) Story
Soft Skills/Workplace Hidden Rules

We learned that the lecture method of teaching was not effective with job seekers, many of whom had struggled in school and were not comfortable with a traditional lecture/note-taking structure. Our training room—so named to reflect the workplace—was set up with round tables rather than desks or tables in a row to avoid any painful reminders of past failures in a school setting.

The modules eventually became interactive, with lots of role playing, group discussion about conflict resolution and attitudes, a mock game show to practice answering interview questions, bingo for building self-confidence, practice interviews with real strangers (usually volunteers from our core employers or board of trustees members), and role playing confrontational situations to develop solutions.

The workshop doesn't require a lot of writing, but job seekers are asked if they would like to read out loud. Occasionally we've identified learning disabilities that way, enabling us to make referrals for help either within Cincinnati Works or with one of our partners.

If job seekers got sleepy during the workshop, the facilitator encouraged them to stand up and walk around so that they became alert, because sleeping on the job wouldn't be tolerated either. Likewise, if a person demonstrated a poor attitude, the leader of the class addressed it on the spot. We took every opportunity to correct behavior that would not be accepted in the workplace, whether it was using a "street" approach when a conflict arose or simply being contrary. The tone of the workshop was all about mutual respect, and the job seekers generally responded well to the environment we created.

The group dynamics were interesting—even fun—to watch. Some groups bonded automatically by lunchtime the first day. Often an informal leader or two emerged and set the tone for the rest of the group. By the end of the week, many groups pitched in and ordered pizza together so they could make plans to meet for their job searches. We loved seeing people looking out for each other, encouraging and supporting their classmates, cheering each other's success, and offering support in the face of disappointments when they came.

Other groups never connected as a team, with members instead working their way through the modules as individuals. The rate of completion among these groups was as high as other groups, but sometimes I couldn't help thinking they were missing out on a potential benefit. Our biggest disappointments, however, came when job seekers failed to finish the workshop, especially when they had made it through the first four days. When people failed to show for the last day, those were the real heartbreakers.

There were three main reasons for dropouts. Some job seekers persisted in unrealistic views of their abilities and their value in the marketplace. They believed they were above an entry-level job. The second reason was that the job seekers found it difficult to make a commitment. They had good intentions but didn't follow through. The final reason was lack of problem solving skills. When their transportation broke down, they didn't know what to do. If their child's babysitter was sick, they had no backup babysitter they could call.

The number of those who completed the workshop hovered at around 90%. We continued to seek to understand the reasons people did not finish so we could improve this number. Our many successes told us we were not naïve in thinking we could adequately prepare someone to go to work within one week's time and that we could change a person's attitudes and behaviors in that short time.

But the workshop was just the beginning. The real work started when the job seeker landed a job.

CHAPTER 8

Advancement: The Dilemma
of the Working Poor

*"We can't become what we need to be
by remaining what we are."*

—Oprah Winfrey

When we started Cincinnati Works, Dave and I wanted to help poor people achieve more than they thought they could achieve in their wildest dreams. Our dream was that our members' children, who saw their parents' hard work and success, would be inspired to reach high too.

By helping willing and capable individuals remove the barriers to their employment, and by supplying them with an ongoing support system, we believed we were setting people up to win. We thought that once we helped the chronically unemployed find and retain employment with an employer who promoted from within, our work was finished. We assumed that our members would automatically position themselves for advancement that would lead to self-sufficiency.

After three years of tracking our members, we found that our assumption was dead wrong. Very few were like Anthony, working multiple jobs and steadily moving on to better paying ones. These disheartening results represented a classic case of our middle class values and assumptions crashing headlong into the reality of generational poverty. About 80% of our members come from families that have long been enmeshed in poverty; only 20% are people in situational poverty—hard times caused by a layoff or a medical crisis, for example.

In early 1999, we reviewed our previous research: In the Greater Cincinnati area, 186,000 adults lived in poverty, of whom 103,000 were able to work if they got assistance in removing their barriers to employment. About 167,000 dependent children were relying on those 103,000 adults to supply their needs. Further study led us to believe that nearly half of those 103,000 able adults—about 50,000—were already working at a part-time or substandard job. However, they were not earning nearly enough to be self-sufficient.

After reviewing the numbers, we were shocked to discover that our hard work had created an outcome we never anticipated. The disappointing truth was that Cincinnati Works was actually increasing the number of working poor in our community. That certainly wasn't our intention, but it's exactly what happened.

Of course, Dave and I were dismayed and puzzled, but we didn't waste time dwelling on our own discouragement. There was too much work that needed to be done. Families' futures depended on how fast we could figure out what was keeping our members from being promoted on the job and getting the raises and benefits they so desperately needed to succeed.

"We've obviously got a gaping hole in our plan to help our members attain self-sufficiency," said Dave. "The numbers are talking to us. We've just got to figure out what they're saying."

"We need to add another phase to our program and focus on advancement," I said, "but our budget doesn't have room for it. Guess I'd better get busy writing grants!" Part of the problem was that, from the very beginning of our organization, we struggled to define what *advancement* meant in concrete terms. Furthermore, we wrestled with how to best create a plan to help our members tap into the financial stability that eluded the majority of them. Most of our members held the simplistic view that advancement meant getting a higher paying job—if the concept of advancement fell within the scope of their thinking at all. We were trying to encourage long-range planning for people who were caught up in crisis mode, trying to survive and make next month's rent. They couldn't think about the future when they were expending so much energy just to make it through today.

Some members understood that the process of advancement could mean a promotion within their current company, or might be helped by acquiring new skills and/or education. We identified some potential funders who, though they were not interested in helping the chronically unemployed, were more than willing to help the working poor in their quest to get ahead. These funders valued the initiative the working poor demonstrated.

Our staff ran two pilot sessions in 1999 that were open to Cincinnati Works members and others in the community who had worked at a full-time job for at least a year but whose salary did not provide self-sufficiency. Each program was composed of three-hour sessions held on four different evenings and covered such topics as choosing career paths, setting financial goals, budgeting, and networking.

We hired an advancement coordinator who developed our new advancement program, which was designed to assist individuals working full-time in accomplishing all of their goals, including helping them discover the job or career that best suited them. Shortly after we moved to our present space, in January 2000, Ohio Governor Bob Taft visited our offices. Amidst much fanfare, he made a few remarks to formally kick off our advancement program.

Candidates for the program were required to complete eight hours of intense, personalized learning in a workshop that was available daytime, evenings, and on weekends in order to accommodate work schedules. The workshop was designed to raise three questions: Where are you now? Where do you want to be? How will you get there?

The workshop, which used materials purchased from WorkNet Publications, started with introspective self-analysis, followed by a general occupational overview. A career planning workbook was supposed to help participants discover their dream jobs and create a path to move toward them. They completed two surveys, one titled "Work Motivation" and the other titled "Preferences/Needs," to help with the process. The last element, called "Effective Problem Solving," was intended to help participants retain their jobs and advance.

Once participants completed the workshop, we asked each individual to meet with the advancement coordinator to develop a career strategy based on the member's needs (improved skills or more education, for example). Just as we did with our members who completed the job retention workshop, we tried to maintain regular contact at three-month, six-month and then one-year intervals to monitor their progress. We also asked them to contact us if they had any change in job status.

By Spring 2001 our city's long-simmering racial tensions reached the boiling point. Fifteen black males under age 40 were killed by police or died in custody between February 1995 and April 2001—some while violently resisting arrest, fleeing, or threatening police. Four police officers were killed or wounded in the course of these encounters. From our inception we had heard stories from our members that demonstrated a fractured relationship between the black community and law enforcement. On March 14, 2001, a group working on behalf of the black men who had died since 1995 and their families combined civil claims against Cincinnati, the police force, and individual police officers into a federal lawsuit. The suit alleged racial profiling, but instead of calling for punitive damages, the lawsuit called for the Cincinnati Police Department to make behavioral changes.

City leaders and the black community were embroiled in emotional discussions about racial tension and police conduct when Timothy Thomas, a black 19-year-old, ran from police, fleeing down a dark alley. He apparently reached to pull up his baggy pants as he was fleeing, but an officer thought he was reaching for a weapon. The officer fired once, and the unarmed teenager was pronounced dead at University Hospital on April 7, 2001. The incident happened in our old neighborhood, Over-the-Rhine. Over-the-Rhine had one of our city's highest crime rates, the average annual income was only $8,600, and more than 90% of the residents subsisted below the poverty level.

Like some of our members, Thomas had racked up numerous misdemeanor charges that triggered arrest warrants. He had amassed 59 misdemeanor charges—primarily for parking tickets, not wearing a seatbelt, and running from police. Tragically, police technology at the time did not tell the officers involved that the outstanding warrants were all for nonviolent crimes.

On April 9 approximately 200 black Cincinnati residents, including Thomas's mother, came to the city council's law and public safety committee meeting, demanding details and accountability for the death of the unarmed youth. The following day hundreds of protesters flocked to the Cincinnati Police District 1 headquarters. By midnight, when the crowd refused to disperse, police officers fired beanbags, tear gas, and pepper spray into the crowd.

The next day the police dispersed a small protest at the corner of Vine and 13th streets. By nightfall, riots began in the business area of downtown Cincinnati, with some looting and small fires. Thankfully, no one suffered serious injuries.

Through it all we continued business as usual. Dave and I never felt unsafe, and we drove downtown to our office daily. Several of our friends were aghast and alarmed, but people needed jobs. From our office window we watched a small group of protesters—mostly young men—disrupting traffic and turning over large flower pots and trash cans, but after a few minutes they moved on, and we went on about our business.

The mayor declared a curfew on the third night of the rioting. This caused anxiety among many of our members who worked second- and third-shift jobs. Our employment support specialists started fielding more and more calls from members who were worried about getting fired because they weren't able to get to their jobs or who were fearful of the violence. Then, on Good Friday—almost miraculously, it seemed to us—the riots stopped.

What never stopped was the determination of our staff and members to keep moving forward, no matter what.

That month we launched a new pilot program called Business Express in partnership with some of our biggest corporate supporters. It was designed to give Cincinnati Works members on-site computer skills and customer service training that would lead to advancement. Candidates had to have held their job for six months or more, possess a clean police record and a high school diploma or GED, and be committed to obtaining the training in order to advance.

One goal was for participants to learn to type 40 words per minute. The typing lab was open three days a week, from noon until 8 p.m., with additional practice times available on two other afternoons. Seventeen people started out in the program. By the end of the pilot, eight people were still participating, and six showed improvement. Still, none had reached the goal of 40 words per minute. The dropouts cited frustration with their slow progress, too many competing obligations, and illness as reasons for their quitting the program.

Business Express was a failure in basically every way. The participants were dismayed at how long it took to make any noticeable progress. Most gave up long before they'd attained sufficient skills to impress an employer. We also learned that employers wanted computer skills that had been proven in the real world. Classroom experience was not enough. Business Express was derailed before it had really gotten started.

On Tuesday morning, September 11, 2001, the office was buzzing with activity. Dave and I were in a board meeting overlooking Race Street. Some of the job seekers were drinking complimentary coffee in the small kitchen, waiting for the second day of the workshop to start. A few people were sitting in the lobby waiting, paging through *Employment Guide*. Our employment support specialists were already at their desks, fielding calls from members and job seekers.

One support specialist's sister called her cell phone and told her about the attack on the World Trade Center. We gathered around the TV in the conference room and watched for some time. I distinctly remember Dave's expression. Normally he cheerily replies, "Outstanding," anytime anyone asks him how he's feeling. I had never seen such grave concern etched on his face before that day—and, thankfully, I haven't seen it since.

Eventually everyone in the office—staff, members, and job seekers—gathered in Sister Jeanne's office, where she led us in prayer. We went on with the workshop—one of the only times we've ever started late—as scheduled that day. Crisis was an everyday event for the people we served, so there was never any question of suspending that week's workshop. We figured the best way we could serve our community and our country was to stay focused on our mission.

As that tumultuous year wound down, nearly 75% of the 159 low-wage earners who started our advancement process had achieved at least one of their goals; however, 8% did not return after the workshop, 23% stopped coming before they reached a goal, and 17% continued to come back but made little or no progress.

A young man named James, who worked for a drive-in, wanted to do something "more," but was unsure what. A test revealed a proficiency in math and science, and he shyly admitted a passion for astronomy. We connected him with a local astronomy society, but he was fearful about doing anything beyond his low-wage job. Our advancement coordinator tried to encourage him to apprentice in a trade or consider college with a major in the sciences. However, James often overslept and missed appointments, and though he always followed up with an apologetic phone call, he continued to be his own worst enemy. The job he knew was less threatening than taking the leap and reaching for the stars.

We learned that our advancement program members were not very different from our job readiness members. They were juggling many responsibilities with poor support systems and too often got pulled back into the struggle of the day-to-day crisis. Their advancement took a low priority when they were struggling to feed their kids or dealing with getting their electricity or phones turned back on.

As we examined the results of the first year, we came to several conclusions:

- Employment stabilization was the critical first step toward advancement.
- Even though people were working, they still faced many of the same barriers that we saw in the unemployed population.
- Our holistic service-delivery system needed to include resources for mental health, legal issues, spiritual guidance, and career counseling, as well as additional help with transportation, childcare, and general healthcare issues.

- Flexible scheduling of all counseling and workshop sessions was critical to adapt to the variety of work schedules.
- The length of time to needed to reach self-sufficiency was usually longer than the two years that we initially anticipated. A more realistic timeframe was 2–5 years, and we learned to expect setbacks along the way.
- Measurable progress indicators included completing a GED, obtaining a driver's license, completing skills training, maintaining contact with the advancement coordinator or an employment support specialist, and following through with the steps outlined in each person's career plan.
- We needed to support and encourage problem solving, creative thinking, time management, and long-range planning.
- Indicators of success included a strong motivation to change, a willingness to commit to the process, and demonstrating the ability to delay gratification.
- Career plans needed to include specific steps with date assignments and a personal accountability plan. Intensive case management was a key to assisting people in following through to reach goals.
- We needed additional information on career opportunities and employment trends in order to expand our members' vision of options.

Shirley Smith, a Cincinnati Works employment support specialist who came to us as a member, offered a lot of insight into this group. She took a keen interest in trying to help other members advance, especially other single moms.

"They've got so many challenges—dropping kids off with different sitters, getting buses, trying to make the dollars stretch," she said at one of our regular Monday staff meetings, "I think another workshop may be asking too much. What they need from us is validation—the support and belief that I never experienced until I came here. They need to hear over and over again, 'Yes, you can do this,' because they aren't hearing it from anybody else. Our members must feel that they are in a place of caring and commitment where we'll walk with them every step of the way on their journey out of poverty."

Some of our earliest contributors and supporters, Mary and Clay Mathile, invited our staff to Dayton to attend a workshop based on the book *Bridges Out of Poverty* by Ruby Payne, Ph.D., Philip DeVol, and Terie Dreussi-Smith. In the workshop Payne emphasized the differences in values among the different classes and the differences in the ways people in different classes think. Until you understand what's important to and valued by people in poverty, your efforts to help break the cycle of poverty will be hampered by misunderstandings and frustration.

Beth and I were elated by what we learned. The book and workshop were a revelation and a turning point for our organization. Payne's approach affirmed what our hearts and our research were telling us about the radically different mindsets and values of the poor versus those of the middle class. For example, while the idea of advancing on the job was fully understood and valued by the middle class, the concept simply didn't translate easily to people in poverty. Therefore, getting them to change their behaviors in order to advance remained difficult at best.

Some of our members had been able to handle a basic, entry-level job despite minimal skills and/or the lack of a high school diploma or GED. They dealt with barriers and became reliable workers. But taking the next step usually required additional skills (especially computer skills) or completion of a certification process. That meant members had to find time in their schedules for additional training.

Often we discovered that any new demands on their schedules required overcoming additional barriers, like a lack of childcare or transportation. The new demands also required problem solving skills to deal with such life events as pregnancy, job injury, car repair, and the stress of debts owed to credit card companies, payday lenders, and loan sharks. Although many members wanted to land a higher paying job or a more satisfying career, the realities of life collided with the steps necessary to achieve advancement, such as filling out additional applications, paying a deposit on a course and showing up for the course, completing a certification, or getting a driver's license.

Compounding the difficulties of advancement for our members was the fear factor. However bad their current situations were, at least their circumstances offered the comfort of familiarity. Getting out of that comfort zone required risk, self-confidence, and the ability to tolerate ambiguity for some period of time. On top of that, many of our members told us that their friends and family were not necessarily enthusiastic about their desire to move ahead.

Still other advancement candidates struggled with poor self-esteem from multiple failures or undiagnosed depression. A lack of time management and multitasking skills often came into play. For others, prior criminal records continued to haunt them. Some could not take the stress and broke down in the face of additional responsibilities.

The working poor trying to move up often got caught in the powerful undertow of the chaos that swirled just below the surface in their lives. Whereas everyday obstacles like a sick child needing to go to the doctor might be an inconvenience for a middle class person, that same event could be the start of a chain of events that mushroomed into a full-blown crisis for our members. This kind of chaos, combined with the fragility of an advancement candidate's struggle for economic independence, often torpedoed even the most tenacious members. Asking them to complete another workshop injected even more stress into their already hectic lives.

We asked everyone on our staff and our board to read *Bridges Out of Poverty*. If we were going to successfully help our members advance, we needed a crash course in the realities of their world.

Around the same time that we were developing the advancement program, the Knowledge Works Foundation approached us about forming a partnership designed to help us with—you guessed it!—advancement. The foundation funded a program called College Works that would allow our members who had stabilized their employment situation an opportunity to attend college. Eligible members received financial assistance for tuition and became members of peer learning groups at Cincinnati State, which did the original assessment, orientation, and registration. The instruction on campus was done in conjunction with Cincinnati Works.

We were elated when the first effort started with eight students.

Shirley Smith, a voracious reader who had enrolled in evening classes at the University of Cincinnati that fall, came to me one afternoon.

"Ruby Payne captures the cycle of poverty perfectly in this book," she said. "The insecurity, feeling inferior. You feel beaten down, limited. You're constantly operating in crisis or survival mode. That thinking is endemic among the poor. Replacing the negative behaviors and responses with appropriate behaviors for the workplace is a long-term process. When you've been in poverty a long time, your memory bank is full of deposits, but they aren't the kind of deposits that you can draw on to move ahead."

Beth and I discussed offering Shirley the job of advancement coordinator after the second person we hired in the course of our first year of the program resigned. Because of Shirley's background, she could relate to the people we were trying to help. She loved to do research—skills honed during all those years of volunteering at her children's schools when she was too afraid to try to get a job.

On the morning of November 27, 2001, I found a spot for my Buick in the parking garage and walked the few short blocks to our office. Oymma Barker, a member we had hired that August to be our new customer service representative, was in tears at the front desk.

"What's wrong, Oymma?" I asked.

"There's been an accident," she said. "Shirley was in the crosswalk heading for her bus when a van ran the red light and slammed into her."

My heart caught in my throat. "Where is she now?"

"They took her to University Hospital."

Shirley was alive, but one leg was so far beyond repair that it needed to be amputated above her knee.

Dave and I were at her bedside soon after she awoke. Her eyes fluttered open, and when she saw us, the first words out of her mouth were, "Do I still have a job with you?"

"Of course you do, Shirley," Dave said in his calm and comforting voice. "Don't you worry about that."

During the next seven months Shirley worked as hard at her rehabilitation as she had at her job. As an employment support specialist Shirley had sometimes juggled more than 40 phone calls a day from members. Because Oymma, in her mid-40s and a member of Class #65, moved from her job as our receptionist/customer service representative to being a support specialist and took on some of Shirley's caseload, she and the other support specialists were able to cover Shirley's workload during her convalescence.

Although we had learned the hard way that hiring job seekers straight out of the workshop was a bad idea, we found that hiring members who had successfully used our program and established themselves in the workplace often worked well. Oymma first came to us after being downsized from J. A. Kendall, where she had sold office supplies for nine years. Her largest account had been Procter & Gamble.

"I put out 72 applications over 10 months and had gone through my 401(k) money," she said. "I was saving my last good pair of dress shoes for interviews only. I'd been steadily employed for 17 years and suddenly found myself in the job market. I'm a single mom and had a son in private school. I was desperate."

The job readiness workshop helped Oymma realize that her anxiety and assertiveness were being misinterpreted as aggressiveness.

"I was at the end of my rope," Oymma said. "Cincinnati Works showed me the error of my ways. My support specialist helped me soften my approach, speech, and presentation. I learned how to do a one-minute interview—an 'elevator statement.'"

Once she applied her new interviewing skills, Oymma got a job at *The Cincinnati Enquirer,* one of our core employers, as an on-call mailer in distribution.

"I have a lot of empathy for the population we serve," she said. "I came here broken. I didn't know what the next step was, but they coached me and gave me hope. We do not enable. We teach and assist for self-sufficiency. That's a thin line. But I believe in the resiliency of people, and I know change is possible."

By March 2002, six of our members planned to start classes at Cincinnati State Technical and Community College through our partnership with the Knowledge Works Foundation. However, by the time classes actually started, our members in attendance numbered zero. We were deflated. The failure of the program was disheartening. Once again we conducted a postmortem in an effort to make sense of yet another failure.

We concluded that we needed clearer communication between College Works, the school, and our organization. Administrative costs relative to direct student services were high, but combining students with a wide range of interests and career goals into groups proved difficult. Exercising time management and multitasking skills was a stretch for our students, given their life challenges. Support systems needed to be better defined from the beginning.

Low-wage earners often became overwhelmed by financially urgent situations. Job loss and old student loans cropped up with alarming frequency and became insurmountable roadblocks. Many students expected instant gratification for their efforts and were easily derailed when they failed to see immediate rewards.

We faced many of the same problems with College Works that we faced with our advancement program. We recommended that Knowledge Works terminate the grant supporting College Works; despite being a superb idea, the reality was that the program wasn't working. Meanwhile, we had big plans for Shirley.

When she arrived at the office in her wheelchair seven months after the accident, Shirley had a new title: advancement resource specialist.

She immediately set about researching local workplaces, individual career paths, and trends in the Cincinnati job market in order to better advise our members on how to fit their career goals into the local economy.

"I looked for high-need jobs and asked what does it take, and is the job doable for our members," she said. Shirley researched fields that paid sufficient wages—$13 to $20 an hour—to enable our members to reach economic self-sufficiency, which we characterized as 200% of the federal poverty level guidelines. She came up with 14 different fields and then identified local companies with jobs commonly available in each of those fields. The jobs that met these criteria fell into four main categories: business, healthcare, skilled trades, and transportation.

Shirley also compiled a list of the training, education, and additional skills and licenses that were needed to advance with all 50 of our core employers and in high-need jobs in the community. "The career verticals get people focused," she said. "We looked at careers where members could get the training they needed in two years or less. For example, in healthcare I knew that dietetic technicians and occupational therapy assistants were in high demand in our area."

We stopped talking to members about "dream jobs" and instead focused on working with them to identify high-wage jobs that suited their educational and skill levels or that were realistically attainable with some assistance from us.

"I wanted to make sure the training was relevant to the local workforce," said Shirley. "Over and over again I've had members come into my office really frustrated and sad because they had gone somewhere and paid for extra training in a field where I could look at the numbers and know they wouldn't find a job.

"There are a lot of so-called schools out there that profit by preying on the career dreams of the poor. One young woman paid thousands of dollars to become a medical technician, but when she applied for jobs, she didn't have the proper licensing or training. She was devastated. My job is to educate our members about what's possible for them and steer them away from scams."

Financial resources for advancement were tight, and we could not afford to waste our funds. We spent about $600 a year for each person in the advancement program.

"Early on about 8% of those in the advancement program had some college, but 31% did not have their GED or high school diploma," said Shirley, who still hoped to complete her own college degree in library science.

We made a lot of changes to our advancement program— some at Shirley's behest and some based on feedback that we'd gleaned from members and our employment support specialists. The biggest change was that we scrapped the workshop. We found that when people are working hard to rise above poverty, they don't have room in their schedules for another workshop. Doing individual career counseling made it more relevant for each person.

We began introducing the idea of advancement during orientation and then again during the job readiness workshop. We also developed a more descriptive definition of self-sufficiency for our members. Our new definition stated that self-sufficiency was when you could provide for the needs of yourself and your family, pay your bills, and put some money in savings with only your paycheck. You do not need food stamps, Medicaid, day care vouchers, or any other type of outside support.

During the workshop the support specialists talked about the first step of advancement: job stability for one year at one job. Then participants worked on one or more of the following:

- A marketable skill
- A certificate or degree
- A driver's license
- A desired behavior

We also shifted the advancement appointments to the same support specialists who had been assigned to our members during the job readiness workshop. That eliminated another time waster since the members didn't have to relate their stories all over again to a new person.

At the first one-on-one meeting with the support specialist, the job seeker was given a pay range goal for self-sufficiency based on the individual's number of dependents. In part this served to get the person to think long-term about the real world. For example, a family of five needs $42,000 per year to be self-sufficient in Greater Cincinnati. These small changes made the process much smoother and helped us retain members who sought advancement. Since its launch in 2000, more than 1,200 people have used the advancement program.

"When you come through the job readiness workshop, there's something emergent that you need," said Beth Smith. "Once you're working, advancement requires longer-range planning, and it's hard to keep that same momentum going."

Shirley embraced her new role: "I help our members make an informed decision about a career so that they can commit. I research all kinds of things—applications for grants or scholarships—to help them advance along their career path."

So how do you measure the worth of helping a single person make it out of poverty?

Always the numbers guy, Dave liked to measure everything. We often discussed the success of our program over the simple meals we ate on our screened-in porch, listening to the waterfall trickle into our pond and watching the birds flit in the shade of the garden filled with flowers that Dave planted according to the seasons.

Our work was slow. There were many setbacks. Sometimes we didn't feel like we came up with answers nearly fast enough. But inevitably, on those rare occasions when we were tempted to be discouraged, we got confirmation that Cincinnati Works was making a difference.

Derrick Mayes, a member of Class #10, continued to stay in touch with Cincinnati Works. He often came in for job search assistance, looking for better positions. He got hired as a part-time flexible mail handler with the U.S. Post Office. There he met Nicole, also a mail handler. They fell in love and had a little girl.

"I wasn't sure what direction to go in terms of my career," he said. "I spent seven years working as a casual/seasonal worker with the city and the post office. I thought I'd go for a career in security."

Dave walked into the small Cincinnati Works break room one afternoon to get a cup of coffee and saw Derrick there.

"Say, Derrick, so when are you going to get married?" Dave asked casually.

"It was like a lightbulb went off in my head," said Derrick, recalling that moment. "I realized that I'm making it. We had bought a three-bedroom, three-bathroom house in Kenwood-Silverton in a safe, comfortable neighborhood a few years ago. We have two cars—high interest rates and all. I'm supporting my daughters. I'm a role model for a lot of people. And besides that, I love Nicole. She always encourages me and helps me do the right thing."

Soon after that, Dave came in with the mail, holding a lovely invitation in his hand. "Guess who's getting married," he said, grinning broadly. "Derrick Mayes, and we're invited."

So, on September 11, 2004, Dave and I, along with Beth and a few others from Cincinnati Works, attended a wedding with 300 other guests at Inspirational Baptist Church in College Hill.

In the receiving line, Derrick grabbed Dave in a big bear hug.

"I cannot thank you enough," he said. "If it wasn't for you and Cincinnati Works, I would not be standing here having this big dream wedding."

I've hardly ever seen Dave cry, but tears glistened in his eyes at that moment when he looked into Derrick's joyful face.

A few years later Derrick went full-time as a mail handler with the post office at $22 an hour with full benefits and a pension fund. In the interim he and Nicole welcomed another daughter.

"We just took our first family vacation ever to Myrtle Beach, and we included my 16-year-old daughter, who plans on being a pediatrician," he said. "Coming from the ghetto in West End, I'm living a dream."

Over the years, our advancement program evolved into a more focused process. We decided that advancement needed to be a one-on-one process because we also recruit underemployed people who have not gone through the Cincinnati Works readiness program and because with a job, they have limited time. An advancement coach works with those in advancement to identify their goals and assess their skills, aptitude, and interests. We are not interested in simply finding members another job; we want to help them find jobs that are satisfying to them as well as allowing them to be self-sufficient.

All advancement members must utilize the services of our financial coach, which helps members develop plans of action that aid them in reaching their goals and achieving self-sufficiency. With the financial coach they work on budgeting, debt resolution, credit building, tax preparation, and more.

Members meet with their advancement coach to explore possibilities considering regional outlook data. The member then looks at real-life possibilities, picks a goal, and makes a plan to achieve it. This plan includes specific steps with dates assigned for completion of each step.

Advancement Schedule

PROGRAM OVERVIEW

Each advancement member, with their advancement coach, will develop and implement an individualized plan to address career, education, financial, and life improvements that will help them reach career growth goals, and ultimately, self-sufficiency.

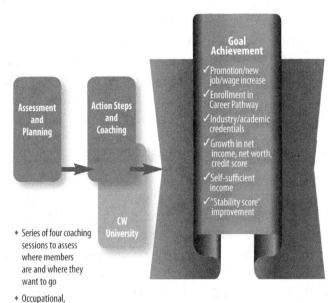

- Series of four coaching sessions to assess where members are and where they want to go

- Occupational, personality, life balance, and financial assessments

- Vision board

- Personal action plan developed to guide further advancement activity

- Member implements action plan

- Ongoing coaching sessions at least every 45 days for motivation, support, problem solving, additional action planning

- CW University classes promote continued growth of personal and professional soft skills and career enhancement skills

←— 4–6 weeks —→   ←———— Varies by individual, 1–5 years ————→

The advancement coach continues to meet with members to make sure they are moving forward with their plans. It takes 6–8 years for most members to reach self-sufficiency because they need to keep their entry-level jobs and take care of their families while devoting the necessary time to working on their goals to reach self-sufficiency.

Susan, manager of advancement services, recently shared with me another story that makes us feel like our efforts are really worthwhile. Violet, who was raised by her aunt and grandmother, is a single mom with one child. She graduated from the job readiness workshop in July 2009 and soon found a job as a teacher's aide for Punkins Patch Learning Center. During this time she completed the State Tested Nursing Assistant program at Great Oaks. Then she was able to secure a job as a patient care aide at Cincinnati Children's Hospital Medical Center.

Violet graduated from Raymond Walters College of Nursing with an associate's degree in April 2013. When she entered the advancement program, her first goal was to pass the nursing boards. Cincinnati Works assisted her in paying the fee required for taking them. After she passed them, Violet was able to obtain her first registered nurse (RN) position at a local hospital, which nearly doubled her wage.

While attending Raymond Walters, Violet worked with her Cincinnati Works advancement and financial coach to improve her credit score. By following her spending plan, she paid off three debts, was approved for a credit-building loan, and was able to establish a residence for herself and her child. By paying off her credit-building loan and making all her monthly payments on time, she earned the $300 matching funds, which she used to pay off her last outstanding debt.

Violet received her Bachelor of Science in Nursing from the University of Cincinnati in December 2015. At the time of this writing, her next goal is to finish a full year of employment in the position she now has and then apply at the University of Cincinnati Medical Center where she can obtain a wider variety of RN experiences. She plans to continue her education in the University of Cincinnati's program for nurse practitioners and to use tuition reimbursement benefits the hospital offers its employees. It has been our pleasure to assist this tenacious woman in achieving her goals.

Some things cannot be proven with numbers alone, and some things are beyond measure. For us, investing in our belief in the indomitable human spirit yields returns that transcend numbers. It's about helping our neighbors—one at a time—and that is a powerful, beautiful thing.

CHAPTER 9

Job Search Purgatory

*"With the new day comes new strength
and new thoughts."*
–Eleanor Roosevelt

The room buzzed with activity and energy. What happened here every Wednesday from 9 a.m. to 1 p.m. represented the heart of what we did: We helped our members find jobs for which they were qualified and where they had a good chance to experience success.

Getting to participate in the job search was the reward for completing the exhaustive week-long job readiness workshop. Job seekers eagerly anticipated getting to this point and were highly motivated by the time they finished the workshop. The graduates of the workshop wanted to test out their new job hunting skills.

By 9 a.m. sharp, the hunt for jobs was already in full swing. Even though Oymma shoved back the folding partition that divided the biggest room we had into a conference room on one side and a teaching room on the other, the large space was still crowded. Our members took up most of the available chairs. This session was pretty evenly divided between women and men. That had become the norm—a far cry from the early days when scarcely any men came through our doors.

Scanning the nearly full room, I guessed that the majority of the job seekers were in their 30s and early 40s. They busily filled out applications, pored over job listings, and took turns surfing the Internet. Most were dressed casually in T-shirts and jeans. A few were dressed in their best interview outfits—just in case. Volunteers were on hand to offer individual job search assistance and help with online applications, faxing, and copying. Involved in many of the activities at Cincinnati Works, our volunteers were businesspeople who were generous with their time and knowledge.

Two women in the job search had been unable to find childcare. A toddler quietly sat in her stroller, looking at a book, while her mom, a woman in her early 20s who looked about six months pregnant, got help with an application from her employment support specialist. Her top did not quite cover her cleavage. Job seekers were told to dress appropriately for interviews, and most complied, but we sometimes had to deal with the subject of inappropriate dress in the workplace. The staff tactfully broached the subject on the occasions when it became necessary. They adeptly helped procure the right clothing from Dress for Success for our female members or from Back on Track for the men.

A small boy around five years old sprawled on the little available floor space, working on a coloring book we kept handy for such occasions. His grandmother filled out an application for a cleaning job at a local hotel.

A mad scramble was on to find a tie for Isaac, a man in his early 40s, to wear to his interview for a job as a security guard. He looked nervous, with a light sheen of sweat on his upper lip. Dave frequently donated ties from the collection he had amassed working so many years in the corporate world.

"You look nice, Isaac," I told him. "Let me see if I can find a spare tie in our office."

A series of catastrophes had left Isaac jobless. He spiraled into a deep depression after months of fruitless job searching before he came to us.

For this occasion he shed his typical T-shirt in favor of a crisp, white-collared shirt that Everly had helped him iron. His hair looked freshly cut.

In the closet I found a stash of pantyhose, but no ties. I also came up empty in the small office Dave and I shared. Glenna took $10 in cash out of the emergency fund we keep for such situations. Off she and Isaac went to the nearby T. J. Maxx to procure an appropriate tie. In addition to purchasing things like ties and pantyhose, the emergency fund also paid for many state identification cards. In the workshop we taught the importance of having two forms of identification—a state ID or driver's license and a Social Security card—and we reinforced this lesson by helping people who didn't have these documents obtain them.

With each member we discussed that person's individual barriers in detail. Some needed additional help with problem solving and with time management, while others needed reminders to pay attention to detail. Some job seekers struggled with low self-esteem and confidence. The support system our job search setting provided was critically important since support from family and friends was a missing ingredient for many job seekers. The job search offered a practical application of all that they had learned during the workshop in a safe, encouraging environment. We enjoyed seeing job seekers progress and celebrated each success with them.

Employment support specialists and volunteers conducted mock interviews during which they learned to realistically and honestly identify and articulate their strengths.

We also dealt with practicalities during job search: Did they need bus tokens to get to interviews? Did they have childcare in place? Did they have an answering machine or voicemail? Did they need any special attire for the interview or once they landed the job? In other words, during the course of the job search we tried to head off any possible problem that a member might encounter.

Shirley, now our advancement resource specialist, entered the room. Oymma and Glenna scrambled to rearrange the bustling room to allow her to maneuver her wheelchair into position next to a working member who was looking for a better job.

Jane had created a detailed but easy-to-read chart that showed all the available jobs at our core employers, along with any special job requirements and the pay range. We used this handy tool to match job seekers to available jobs. She divided the employers into such categories as security, transportation, social service/healthcare, food service, environmental/ general labor, and professional. Today the job coaches use Salesforce case management tools.

When job seekers first came to Cincinnati Works, some had an unrealistic view of the jobs that were out there. More than a few came through the door with the notion that they wanted an office job where they could wear nice clothes, but they didn't have the computer skills or basic phone system knowledge required for entry-level customer service jobs. They also quickly discovered that a large percentage of the jobs available at the entry level were second or third shift. Throughout the workshop we gently steered job seekers toward realistic and achievable goals. And yet, at the job search stage, we still found some who engaged in wishful thinking and needed coaching to adjust their ambitions to reflect the job market they were attempting to enter. Getting a person to focus on jobs within his or her grasp required our support specialists to strike a delicate balance: They provided healthy doses of reality mingled with generous dollops of encouragement.

We often asked our job seekers, "How many of you enjoy job searching?"

Nobody ever raised a hand.

We assured them that few people, including the Cincinnati Works staff, enjoyed the job search process, no matter what position they were seeking. Searching for a job was the pits, and we all understood. Luckily, this stage in the process was a partnership, and many of us had "been there."

Preparation for the job search began in the workshop. A great deal of time was spent on filling out applications properly and completely, including the use of references and proper listing of job history.

Although we taught a module on the interview process, we found that the best technique for teaching this skill was to use actual practice and to let others watch their peers as they practiced. In addition to our team members, we had volunteers who came in to conduct mock interviews from 1 p.m. to 4 p.m. on Wednesday afternoons after job search.

Since we knew that interviewing was stressful for our members, we devoted many hours to developing interviewing skills. Our core employers, board members, and retired local executives were generous with their time and assisted with these sessions. By practicing with a variety of interviewer personalities, the job seeker would be prepared for any style of interview. Though these trial runs were stressful, our members consistently told us that having an opportunity to test their interviewing skills was one of the most useful parts of our process.

While in the workshop, job seekers filled out questionnaires related to the schedule they were able to work, their education, their police records (if applicable), whether they had a driver's license, their work history, and their computer skills (if applicable). When this information was collected and some good matches for the candidate were noted, the job seeker began the job search in earnest. On the first day of the job search, we provided the job seeker with hot job leads. These leads, along with the continuously updated list of available jobs, helped the job seeker to identify an industry that interested her or him.

The employment support specialists carefully went over the applications that members started on Friday in the workshop. Many of the job seekers were shocked to learn how quickly they would be eliminated as a job candidate due to a mistake or missing information on the application. Our core employers told us that applications with missing information and glaring errors ranked among their biggest pet peeves.

During the job search the employment support specialists and volunteers also helped job seekers fill out applications online if they were available. Sometimes we had employers' applications on file so that we could go over them with applicants. We checked for misspellings and incomplete information, anything that would give a human resources person a reason to put that application into "the circular file"—the wastebasket.

The employment support specialists scheduled all appointments for interviews with our core employers. The job seekers scheduled other interviews on their own, with some interviews obtained using cold-calling techniques learned in the workshop. For higher-level jobs, a team member met with the job seeker for a pre-screening session in order to give the job seeker some insight about the job, the salary, and the company. Job seekers could also request a pre-screening session if they felt unprepared for their interview. This step helped people anticipate the employer's concerns and eliminate them, especially when the applicant had legal issues or a poor work history.

With all the needed tools in place, the job seeker began the interview process. We got feedback when the interview was with a core employer. This information allowed us to debrief the job seekers and coach them so that they could be more successful in subsequent interviews. Another part of the preparation was to teach the job seekers to ask questions during the interview to make sure the job was a good fit, which was critically important for retention.

Jodie, our legal services coordinator, stepped in to deliver good news to one of the youngest members, Jebron, age 19. "Legal Aid has agreed to take on your case," she said.

A wide smile spread over Jebron's face. "So, Miss Jodie, you really think I got a good shot at getting that off my record?"

"Yes, I do. Now come into my office so we can talk about the next steps."

The lanky teenager jumped up and followed her out of the room.

In the course of the workshop, Jebron, who talked a mile a minute and appointed himself a class leader, finally admitted that he had trouble reading. Afraid of failing at something again, he was reluctant to pursue a GED, which would make him eligible for a better job.

About 40% of our members had criminal records, and about 25% were dealing with a current legal issue—child custody problems, landlord troubles, consumer debt, domestic violence, or a combination—that they needed help resolving.

We knew we needed a legal services advocate on staff, so we hired Jodie, who was in her last semester of law school. Jodie found that often our members had misdemeanors that were automatically upgraded to felonies because they failed to show up in court or pay the fine for some minor offense. Maybe the notice got lost in the mail due to their frequent moves, or maybe they ignored the initial charge because they didn't have the money or because they were afraid. Either way, having a felony on their record effectively knocked job seekers out of consideration for the majority of jobs that our core employers offered. We discovered that 8–10% of our members were eligible to have their records expunged because they had been convicted of only one felony, and the felony was nonviolent in nature.

However, the odds were that even if our members with a single felony on their records had realized their eligibility for expungement, virtually none would have had the patience and wherewithal to navigate the laborious and complex legal process required to get their records expunged.

During their first job search session, all job seekers with criminal records scheduled an appointment with our legal coordinator to become better prepared to talk about their legal issues at an interview. In the workshop and during job search, our staff members and volunteers from core employers coached each person individually on exactly how and when to address anything on his or her record. They were taught to accept responsibility for their actions and to communicate what they learned from the experience and why they would be good employees. It is still true that without legal services, we would be unable to assist many job seekers.

We started talking about core employers at orientation so that the people we were helping knew whom we worked with and the kinds of jobs we knew about. Some job seekers were frustrated and lacked self-confidence because in the past they had applied for jobs for which they were not qualified. For example, someone with a history of theft was ineligible for a job at a financial institution. Not being aware of factors like this, many members had been rejected repeatedly and got discouraged. We assisted them in applying for jobs for which they did qualify.

Sometimes the employers and the jobs being offered were not what the members were looking for and they quit the workshop. Over the years we've come to expect that about 20% of those who start the week in the workshop will not complete it for a variety of reasons.

What surprised us was that some members successfully completed the workshop but did not show up for the job search. Almost 10% of the people who stuck it out and successfully completed our intensive, 30-hour job readiness workshop never took the crucial next step with us. We just had to hope that they took what they learned in the workshop and applied it to their own independent job searches.

On this particular morning, like most Wednesday mornings, two of the graduates from last week's workshop were missing from the hubbub. They likely wouldn't ever come through the elevator doors on our floor again. As much as all of us tried to stay on an even keel at all times, each time a newly graduated member failed to show up for the job search was a blow. Watching a person walk away from what you know is likely their best chance to rise above poverty was heart-wrenching for our staff—especially for the employment support specialist assigned to that person. But we could not afford to dwell on those who chose to give up. Too many other members counted on us to be fully present and upbeat for them. And, on our own staff, Oymma Barker served as a living, breathing reminder that every once in a while someone who initially disappeared after going through the workshop would eventually return.

Why would someone sit through an entire week of a rigorous job readiness workshop, submit to a drug screen and police background check, and then not look for a job? The answer to that question continued to elude us.

Myriad excuses cropped up. Workshop attendees blamed health issues—usually dubious since they were never mentioned until the job search was slated to begin. Some claimed the jobs that they wanted required a high school diploma or GED that they didn't have, and they didn't want the jobs that took workers without diplomas or GEDs. Still other workshop attendees claimed that a newly discovered or troubled pregnancy made the job search inconvenient.

Whatever the excuse, we have heard them all. Unfortunately, we don't have many like Oymma come to us that second time. All we could do was throw a lifeline out and hope against hope that the poor would have the strength to grab it and hold on.

In late April 2006, Oymma was walking down the hallway preparing to teach her segment of the workshop when she coughed and threw her hand to her chest. She felt a lump. Immediately she went to Jacque's office and asked her if she had reason to be concerned. "Call the doctor right now," Jacque urged. Oymma made an appointment right away. She was diagnosed with breast cancer.

Over the next few months our staff rallied around Oymma, bought her meals when she was too sick from chemotherapy to cook for herself, and generally made sure she was okay. "I knew my coworkers felt like family, but I was unprepared for the outpouring of love and kindness they showed me," she said. "They thought of everything and just kept giving. Once I came back to work, on some days I had zero energy. People bent over backwards to make sure I was okay. We really are family here."

One afternoon in the break room, a woman who was missing all her front teeth caught my attention. Her short hair looked like it hadn't been brushed. She wore a faded, baggy T-shirt and appeared to be about my age—in her 60s—but I guessed she was probably 10 or 15 years younger than she looked. Years of hard living were heavily etched on her face. I wondered if she was Appalachian and how she had lost her teeth.

I learned that she'd worked in a factory for eight years but she was laid off when a truck smashed head-on into her 10-year-old compact car. After the accident she was no longer able to do the repetitive factory work—or even to remember the steps of the job—that she had done for years.

She faithfully showed up for the job search week after week, smiling and hopeful. Brief conversations in the small break room where workshop attendees and members ate lunch revealed enough for me to know that it was likely she had suffered some sort of brain damage. I admired her determination. She rooted for her fellow class members as they secured jobs one by one. I rooted for her.

The Appalachian women who completed the workshop but failed to show up for the job search usually did so after their husbands or boyfriends threatened to beat them for joining Cincinnati Works and trying to enter the workforce. Some Appalachian men in poverty considered having their spouses or girlfriends working outside the home to be an affront to their manhood and viewed outsiders like us with great suspicion. It was very disheartening to see these women drop out after coming so far. They were terrified for their safety or were unwilling to risk being outcasts in their close-knit community—or both.

Although Appalachians represented about half of the population living in poverty in our area, they were one group that we found almost impossible to reach. But we were determined to keep trying. We didn't give up just because something was hard. How could we when we ask our members not to give up?

All of our members had stories to tell, but we didn't push them for any details unless they were vital to the job search. Of course, we listened if they volunteered information, but a big improvement came in 2000 when we changed our process so that each member stayed assigned to the same employment support specialist. That way a person only had to tell his or her story one time. This new process also helped foster a bond of trust with the support specialist.

That change was a small step toward restoring dignity to people who had often been required by the system to share painful and humiliating events over and over again with all sorts of social services personnel, a process that only added to their trauma.

Another reason job seekers dropped out of the job search was lack of motivation. Often they were living with a relative or friend, or they were receiving public assistance. An individual would attend our workshop simply to satisfy a family member or fulfill a requirement that made them eligible for some sort of government assistance.

Jacque, our behavioral and mental health counselor, suspected that alcoholism was the root of the problem for almost half of that 10% who didn't follow through and search for a job. And alcohol abuse went hand in hand with the fog of depression. Although we screened all potential members for illegal drug use, detecting a drinking problem was far more difficult.

The primary culprit that kept these workshop attendees from seeking employment was their own low self-esteem, which led to self-sabotage. Virtually all of them were used to living in crisis mode, going from one high drama to the next. Like Shirley Smith once was, they were paralyzed by a fear of failure because they had been rejected over and over again. They didn't feel good enough about themselves to believe that they "deserved" to get their lives together. Although our employment support specialists called and followed up, bolstering the self-esteem of people who had been repeatedly stripped of dignity by the dependency system society had created proved difficult. At times a member's own self-doubt was the one barrier that was insurmountable.

Everly, our employment coordinator, and Jodie were scrambling. Everly was on the phone with a core employer who called to alert us that the woman he interviewed the previous week for a customer service job hadn't shown up for her first day of work. While Everly had him on the phone, Jodie called Loretta, a single mom in her 30s, at home. She answered on the first ring.

"I didn't think I was gonna get that job," she explained, sounding defensive. "They offered me one on the spot when I went into Popeye's. It's just down the street, so I think it's better for me."

While Everly was on the other line trying to determine whether the employer would be open to giving the errant job seeker a second chance, Jodie patiently explained to Loretta why the job with our core employer offered far more upside potential than the job down the block at the fast food restaurant.

After several minutes Jodie said in a resigned voice, "I understand your position. Let us know if you want to come back in." We had learned that pushing and cajoling members into taking a job they didn't want rarely resulted in job retention.

Moments like that one were tough on everyone—the job seeker, the core employer, and our staff. We wove a delicate web of trust in the business community. When one of the threads was broken, it hurt everybody. We screened candidates carefully before sending them to core employers. We strove to send the most qualified job seekers we had. There was no obligation on the employer's part to hire a Cincinnati Works job seeker, but we asked that the people we sent be given consideration. Over the years we built a strong, hard-won reputation within the business community. We took every success and failure equally to heart because we have built a family with our members. What each and every member does or doesn't do counts.

In order to protect the relationship with our core employers, we put several practices into place. Besides mock interviewing, we required pre-screening for interviews with some core employers. We wanted to be convinced that the person was legitimately interested in that job. We adhered to a "one strike and you're out" policy. If someone quit or got terminated from a core employer job, they would not get a second chance at any of our core employers for a period of three months. In the interim we would place them with a company that was not a core employer if we could.

The employment support specialists always tried first to place a job seeker with a core employer, but sometimes we found that the individual did not qualify for any of those positions, core employers with suitable jobs were not hiring, or the job seeker did something that caused them not to be hired. On average a job seeker went through 2.3 jobs before that person became stable in the workplace, which meant we needed an alternative job search method. We called it "open job search." Shirley kept a packet that detailed the job requirements of employers that weren't part of our group of core employers.

The vital information about each job was highlighted so the job seeker could quickly spot possible jobs and find the employer contact information. They could fax a resume or make an inquiry by phone immediately, but since they were looking for jobs where we had no relationship with the employer, the support specialists didn't make contact with the potential employer. Open job search required that the job seeker take the lead. It was a completely individual approach, and the process continued as long as the job seeker was actively searching. Job searching usually took 4–6 weeks, depending on how aggressive the job seeker was and how many barriers the person had.

If the job seeker became stuck, we employed an alternative service plan. The job seeker was asked to bring back a note after going to an interview, or we asked him or her to make an appointment with Jacque, our on-site mental health and behavioral counselor, to pinpoint the problem. The support specialists stopped working with job seekers who didn't complete their assignments. If this approach failed to yield results within a three-month period, the job seeker was placed on the "inactive" list. To reactivate their memberships, they had to meet with Jacque again. During that interview she evaluated whether changes in circumstances would help them to succeed. We constantly worked to instill the idea that Cincinnati Works was only the coach; the job seeker was the player in the game.

CHAPTER 10

Take This Job and Shove It

"Our greatest glory is not in never failing,
but in rising up every time we fail."
–Ralph Waldo Emerson

Darren Thigpen, an employment support specialist, heard the tension in the member's voice over the phone.

"I don't know how much more of this guy's racist junk I can take, Darren," said the man, who had finally landed a job picking up trash for the city after a six-week job search. "A supervisor shouldn't be doing that stuff. Who does he think he is, jawin' off at me like that? I'm reaching my boiling point."

"Hang in there," Darren replied calmly. "I'm sorry he's acting like that. Who knows why? What I'd like you to focus on right now is that you are coming up on your one-year anniversary in that job. You've had great reviews. I imagine you'll be in a position to get a better job soon. Besides, aren't you and your wife expecting your fourth child?"

Darren—an African American who grew up in the affluent, predominantly white suburb of Wyoming, Ohio—joined us on July 5, 2005. Darren's mother was a registered nurse. His father was a Morehouse man and a human resources executive with Procter & Gamble. His first brush with the sort of violence more common to poor neighborhoods came when he was in seventh grade: His favorite cousin was shot in a restaurant bathroom in Milwaukee. "I saw how that affected the family. They never recovered," said Darren.

After getting his degree in English literature and communications from Central State Wilmington College, where he had a basketball scholarship, Darren, eager to make a difference, went into education. Eventually he landed what he considered a dream job: a position as a case manager at Project Succeed Academy, a special charter school in downtown Cincinnati that worked with some of the poorest kids in the city.

However, he was dismayed when his contract wasn't renewed. "I was more hurt than I acknowledged at the time," said Darren, who has a young son and a teenage daughter. "I passed on some jobs, and before I knew it 10 months had gone by."

He lapsed into a depression. The turning point came when he received a letter from his mother and father. "My mother wrote: 'We've taught you a lot, and you know a lot. We don't know why you aren't out there using it. If your life isn't what you want, find a way of turning a negative into a positive,'" recalled Darren.

The following Sunday at church, Everly, who worked in advancement, mentioned the employment support specialist position at Cincinnati Works to Darren. "In retrospect I think me going without a job happened for a reason," said Darren. "I know the temptation of losing yourself in *Sports Zone* or Xbox 360. I see it from a whole different perspective."

In the cubicle next to Darren's, Oymma tried to calm down a frantic young woman who was threatening to quit her new job as an administrative assistant. Recently promoted to team leader for the employment support specialists and a Cincinnati Works member herself, Oymma listened while the woman talked about her boss, an entrepreneur who owned his own small company.

"He yelled at me for 20 minutes this morning because I couldn't find a file, but that was something the other woman misfiled back in April before I ever even got there," she said, crying. "I can't take this crazy place."

"How about if Everly and I come down there later today?" Oymma asked soothingly. "We'll sit down with you and your boss and discuss expectations. I know it's hard right now, but I really think this can work out."

This employer wasn't one of our core employers, and he did have a reputation for being hard on people. The member had been a nurse's assistant for several years until she injured her back on the job. She came to us after six months of fruitlessly seeking an office job on her own.

By the time Oymma hung up the phone, the woman had calmed down and agreed to hang on. Oymma had scarcely taken a breath before the phone rang again.

How many times have you had this thought? *I ought to just quit.* Most of us have entertained that notion at some point in our work lives but never acted upon it. Unfortunately, many of our members have done exactly that. In the heat of the moment or in the face of a problem—real or imagined—they quit on the spot, failing to grasp how critical job retention is to their future.

From the outset of Cincinnati Works we were astonished by how many different definitions there were in our industry for job retention. Even the leaders of job programs didn't agree on its meaning. Some programs claim successful job retention if someone holds a job for one month. Others set the bar at three months or six months. At one seminar we attended an example was given where an organization's retention rate varied from 38% to 96%, depending on how retention was defined. At the same seminar we were told that retention was what an organization said it was. We were flabbergasted by that declaration.

Almost 10 years after we started Cincinnati Works, still no standard had been established, which made comparing the retention rates from different programs virtually impossible. Early on we decided to use two definitions of retention because we had two groups of customers: the members and the employers.

Statistics showed that if someone kept working, even if it was with more than one employer, that individual would probably stay out of poverty. But the employer's concern was whether that member continued with the same company. Therefore, we measured the retention rate by whether the member had been working at least one year *and* whether the person had remained at the same company for a full year. We also concentrated on increasing the length of time a person stayed at one company because holding down turnover costs was vital for employers. We also learned that helping members stabilize in a single workplace made it more likely that they would successfully advance and thereby reach self-sufficiency faster.

Starting in the workshop, we emphasized the importance of retention with the job seekers. Such modules as "Conflict Resolution," "Attitudes and Beliefs," and "The Hidden Rules of the Workplace" addressed issues that would jeopardize retention.

Jacque usually led the module on conflict resolution. One morning she walked into the room where a dozen job seekers sat at the round tables. All had been on multiple job interviews, and some were visibly discouraged. They had been referred to us by the Bridgework program, the Salvation Army, and one woman's son had suggested she try Cincinnati Works.

Jacque announced, "On every job you are going to have conflict. Where does conflict start? Conflict starts within you. It's about perception. You have the power to determine whether you have a pleasant or unpleasant interaction.

"Conflict originates and germinates between here and here," she continued, pointing to her head and heart. "Do you do things just because of how you were raised? We learn from our environment. Identify your weakness before you get into the workplace. Is it office gossip? Ego issues? Problems with authority? Let them fall. They are not important at the end of the day."

One job seeker said, "My niece always seems to be in some kind of drama. She's had five jobs in the last few months, and everywhere she goes there's a problem."

"What do you think the common denominator is?" Jacque asked. "I'll tell you what it is: drama. Either she's bringing it or she's gravitating to it. And it's because she doesn't feel good about herself. It's not the employers' fault. If we grew up in a hellish household, we have a tendency to allow ourselves to be drawn to that kind of drama.

"I grew up in the hood. I've seen a lot of examples of people putting themselves in a box. Maybe your teacher or your mama told you that you were too fat, too ugly, too dumb, too whatever to get a certain job. Some people are afraid of success. Responsibility comes with success. Everybody successful has failed. Patti LaBelle was told she was too black, her voice was too high, and her nose was too big to ever make it as a singer."

She paused and then asked, "What ticks you off?"

"Racial slurs."

"Stereotypes."

"Mean attitudes."

"People do things to get other people angry," said Jacque. "When you get into a victim's mentality, that mindset is self-defeating. Don't listen when your coworker says, 'That boss don't care about you,' or allow yourself to think, 'You're just trying to be against me.' Don't succumb to anybody's foolishness. We can gain mastery over anything we want to try.

"Conflict management is all about trying to come to a consensus. Sometimes you have to agree to disagree."

Kyra, a woman in her mid-20s, said, "Sometimes on my old job I got mad because one of my coworkers was always disrespecting me, and that's one thing I can't stand."

Jacque smiled and replied, "I hear that a lot. Respect is important, but let's think about that. When you feel like somebody is disrespecting you, is that a good reason to quit a job? And what if it's the boss?"

"I don't ever put up with disrespect out of nobody," said Jeffrey, an older man, shaking his head for emphasis.

"All the training I've ever gotten from other programs has been about getting a job," said a woman named Candy. "But I think what you're teaching us is more about performing in order to keep a job day in and day out."

"That's right," said Jacque. "Work isn't about instant gratification. You have days that are not that great. Sometimes you work with people you don't like. And I can guarantee you your boss is not always going to say 'please' and 'thank you.'" That comment brought laughter and nods of recognition.

Later that afternoon Sarah, who served on our employer board, and Bill, both representatives from the human resources department of an area health system with seven hospitals, stopped by to talk with the class about employers' expectations and the interview process.

"We're here because we'd love to see more Cincinnati Works people get hired this year," said Sarah. "As you probably know by now, we operate under some of the strictest rules of any of Cincinnati Works' core employers because we deal with children and the elderly. Patient safety is paramount. That means we cannot hire anyone with a violent past or a history of theft. The other difficulty is that the laws that govern who we can and cannot hire change all the time." She thanked the group for the opportunity to share from the recruiter's point of view. "I'm here to help you understand what goes on inside an organization during the hiring process," she said.

Our core employers told us that they liked interacting with our job seekers in a setting where they could let their guard down and help a group of people who were eager to use their skills. "Of course, how you present yourself initially is important," Sarah said. "How fast you return phone calls and how you dress. The dress at our hospitals and offices is business casual, but some people come to an interview looking like they're going to a club. Scrubs are okay, but don't wear cutoff shorts and flip-flops."

Bill added, "Maintain a good work history. Big gaps are a real turnoff for an employer. Stick to a job and build credibility and responsibility. It's also important to be honest. If you have a shaky work history, tell us why you were discharged."

One woman raised her hand. "Can you give us some interview tips?"

"Sure," Sarah replied. "Be sure you have voicemail or an answering machine, and check it frequently. People who are looking to hire for a position expect you to call back promptly. Keep your greeting simple on your voicemail—just your name and that you'll get back to the caller. I don't want to hear a philosophical statement, a Bible verse, or thumping music when I call you. When you leave a message for me, say your name slowly and clearly, and leave your phone number clearly. Do those simple things and you'll stand out. As an employer, I see so many applicants who don't have it together."

Once job seekers became full-fledged Cincinnati Works members, each was given a copy of our "Call Before You Quit" policy, which we borrowed from the No One Is Unemployable program. We asked all new members to sign and keep the pledge. All of our staff emphasized the idea that Cincinnati Works should be thought of in the same way as 411—in other words, a source of information as opposed to the emergency nature of 911. We created an atmosphere of kindness, respect, and support so that members would come to us if they needed help solving a problem—before it turned into an emergency.

Call Before You Quit
Cincinnati Works is an organization that assists individuals in finding and keeping full-time jobs.

WHAT is the policy?

- Call Before You Quit means that you will call your employment support specialist before you quit any job.

WHY do we have this policy?

- This is the last time that we want you to have to search for a job without already having one.

- We want you to be able to build your work history, earn a steady income, plan your budget, and avoid leaving a job before you have another one lined up.

- By calling your support specialist, you will give yourself the opportunity to talk through your options before you make a decision.

WHEN should you call?

- Call your support specialist before you quit or before your actions cause you to be terminated.

Suggestions:

- Call your support specialist anytime there are things that bother you about your job.

- Call the first time your supervisor, your coworkers, your customers, or your duties upset, confuse, or frustrate you.

- Call before your frustration results in your missing any days of work, which could cause you to be terminated.

- Call the first time your day care or transportation plans seem not to be working.

- Call before things go completely down the tubes.

WHAT if I don't Call Before I Quit?
If you choose not to Call Before You Quit, and you would like
to continue to receive job search assistance from Cincinnati
Works, you will have to:

1) Call your support specialist to schedule a "debriefing
   session," which may involve problem solving and
   conflict resolution seminars and a renewal of your
   commitment to stay in touch with your support
   specialist.

2) Participate in activities assigned by your support
   specialist.

Your Pledge:

- I understand that Cincinnati Works wants to help me
  stabilize in the workforce and limit the number of
  interruptions in my work history.

- I promise to call my employment support specialist
  before I quit or before my actions cause me to be
  terminated from any job.

- I understand the consequences if I do not Call Before
  I Quit any job.

Name _____ Date _____

Old habits die hard: Not all of our members remembered
their pledge when something started going south. Some of
the hardest situations arose when we didn't learn about the
problem until it was too late.

Experience taught us that it took at least one year for a
member to stabilize in a job, so our retention services followed
a strict regimen for the first year. For example, job loss was

most likely to occur in the first three months. Maybe a bus route changed, a car broke down, or a childcare provider closed her doors. Maybe the job wasn't a good fit in the first place. For example, an older member with arthritis took a job where he was subjected to extreme cold in a freezer at a meatpacking company, which aggravated his condition.

When a member secured employment, the employment support specialist asked three key questions: Was the person eligible for Earned Income Tax Credit? Was he or she required to report employment to the Department of Jobs and Family Services to keep from being sanctioned? If the person lived in subsidized housing, had he or she reported the change in income as required?

During that three-month trial period, the support specialists tried to maintain frequent communication with both the member and the employer to troubleshoot and offer support. Staying in touch was difficult because the people we served often changed phone numbers and residences. If the member remained noncommunicative during those three months, he or she was deemed inactive. Once a support specialist put a member on the inactive list, the member was required to attend a debriefing session to review what had happened, what the member's responsibility was in the situation, and what would be different next time. In other words, it became a teaching/learning moment to improve future outcomes. This session and the follow-through on the recommended plan were necessary in order to receive our services again.

After that first year, services were provided as needed. The following are the steps in the retention strategy for the first year.

Retention Strategy

Month 1

Week 1
- Office manager generates letter of congratulations
- Employment support specialist makes Week 1 contact (phone, message, or mail)
- Employment coordinator contacts employer to get supervisor's name and telephone number, and to explain the role of Cincinnati Works and the support specialist

Week 2
- Support specialist makes site visit or meets with member near workplace (within first month of work)
- If visit is not possible, support specialist makes Week 2 contact (phone, message, or mail)

Week 4
- Support specialist contacts member to do a 30-day evaluation
- Support specialist contacts supervisor to exchange feedback

Month 2
- Month 2 contact #1
- Month 2 contact #2
- Support specialist contacts supervisor to exchange feedback

Month 3
- Month 3 contact #1
- Month 3 contact #2
- Support specialist talks to member about advancement
- Support specialist contacts supervisor to exchange feedback

Month 4
- Month 4 contact #1
- Month 4 contact #2

Month 5
- Month 5 contact #1
- Month 5 contact #2

Month 6
- Month 6 contact #1
- Month 6 contact #2
- Support specialist contacts supervisor to exchange feedback

Month 7
- Month 7 contact #1

Month 8
- Month 8 contact #1

Month 9
- Month 9 contact #1
- Support specialist contacts supervisor to exchange feedback
- Revisit member's advancement potential:
  Client not an advancement match

  Client is an advancement match
    – Support specialist continues retention strategy
    – Support specialist makes an appointment to review advancement goals

Month 10
- Month 10 contact #1

Month 11
- Month 11 contact #1

Month 12

- Month 12 contact #1
- Send member letter of congratulations for being employed one year
- Change the person's status to "employed" or to "advancement" if they are working toward their advancement goals
- Change the person's status to "inactive" if they have no interest in advancement

Some members don't find the job a good fit and may choose to seek another one. It may take two or three tries for some, but the retention support system is in place to stabilize them and keep them employed.

During the workshop we also presented job seekers with a pledge called "Core Employers Are Important." By reading and signing this sheet, they signified that they understood how important our core employers were to our success and the consequences for poor behavior at interviews and after employment. The reputation of Cincinnati Works was on the line: A bad experience with one of our members could jeopardize job possibilities for future members.

Members who made major mistakes with core employers made it tough for us to help them. Darren worked with a 27-year-old man who had grown up in foster care downtown. "We nicknamed him 'Big Baby,' because he was six-foot-four but would become very emotional during the workshop," recalled Darren. "He broke down crying in the hallway due to a situation with his six-year-old son and the boy's mama." First Darren helped him land a job in security, but then he got hurt on the job. Next he got a job cleaning for Cincinnati Children's Hospital. One afternoon while he was stripping some sheets, he pricked himself on a needle. He filed a lawsuit against the hospital and lost his job.

He called Darren on a Friday afternoon, crying and telling Darren that he was thinking he might as well try selling drugs on the corner. "I tried to do this legit," he said.

"If you do that, think about your son," urged Darren. "He'll go back to his mother or end up in foster care. Are you willing to risk him going through what you went through?"

Darren held out hope that the man would pull it back together: "He'd gotten stabilized and gained custody of his son. He's a talented rapper, but he's starting to make excuses. Everything is always everybody else's fault. It's going to be really hard to help him find something else until he takes responsibility. The jury is out on him."

The feedback we got from our core employers helped tremendously with job retention by giving us vital information that we used to coach our members to become better employees. We could often salvage a job if we knew about a situation early on and could work with the member and the employer to defuse it.

Terms for Working with Core Employers
Because the core employers are so important to Cincinnati Works, every member is asked to sign an agreement that stipulates the terms of working with them. In it they agree to:
- Be pre-screened for all core employer positions
- Show up for all core employer appointments and arrive on time
- If hired, to meet or exceed the employer's expectations

- Give written permission for Cincinnati Works to confer with their supervisor
- Stay on the job for at least a year

Members may lose access to the core employer opportunities or have them suspended for a time.
Possible infractions are:
- Not showing up for an interview
- Being late for an interview without proper notice
- Inappropriate behavior during an interview
- Inappropriate dress for an interview
- Failing a drug screen
- Submitting false information on an application
- Failing to show up to start a job
- Termination (for any reason)
- Quitting prior to one year on the job

For the first infraction, the consequences are:
- Debriefing with the employment support specialist
- Suspension of core employer services for at least three months
- Counseling may be required to lift the infraction

For the second infraction:
- Debriefing with support specialist
- Suspension of all employment services until member has kept the same job for one year
- Counseling may be required to lift the infraction

If accused of theft or any illegal activity at a core employer, services with core employers are permanently suspended.

There is a workshop every week either at our main office or one of our satellite offices. Each of the employment support specialists rotates, taking a new group of trainees through the workshop. They work with those individuals to prepare them for the job search process. In that same period, they follow up on all the previous trainees who are already working. In contrast, job seekers in the Phoenix and Next Step programs work with a dedicated support specialist. More on those programs later in the book.

When care is taken to maintain the relationship with core employers, the dividends are great. Our employment coordinator frequently received letters like this one from The Christ Hospital in Cincinnati:

> *The Christ Hospital places great value on community employment partnerships. The human resources team at The Christ Hospital has numerous relationships throughout Greater Cincinnati that it continues to develop and grow. Across all these relationships, helping applicants understand and meet employer expectations regarding the recruitment and onboarding process is particularly important in order for the match to be successful.*
>
> *The Christ Hospital has benefited greatly from the partnership with Cincinnati Works and believes the quality of candidates presented is well aligned with our recruitment vision. Teelisha Higgins, HR coordinator for The Christ Hospital, reinforced this message at her recent visit at Cincinnati Works. She stressed the importance of an accurate and complete employment*

application, including work history, reason for leaving, and up-to-date contact information: "It's important applicants understand how to best present their qualifications and to separate themselves from the large number of other applicants. I feel my role in successfully partnering with our community resources includes coaching and mentoring our potential workforce so they can have the best possible opportunity."

During one particular session, the question was posed to Teelisha regarding criminal background check issues being an automatic disqualifier for employment. "We look at the whole recruitment picture, including the behavioral interview, technical interview, pre-employment drug screen, and reference and criminal background checks. Particular to the criminal background check, both frequency and how recent are relevant to employers and are reviewed very thoroughly. It's important to be upfront and honest about your background, both employment and criminal records." Teelisha continues, "A strong, continuous work history also helps present a good impression to potential employers. Be able to explain any gaps or issues around your departure from previous employers."

The Christ Hospital has appreciated the consistency of the caliber of applicants provided through the partnership with Cincinnati Works and looks forward to continued success stories.

In an effort to better understand the needs of employers, we established an Employer Advisory Committee made up of representatives from some of our core employers. The committee helped design a survey that assessed our strengths and weaknesses in preparing members for employment with core employers. They continue to advise us on hiring trends, new HR practices, and existing best practices. They also help us to get feedback directly from hiring managers on other various topics.

New barriers, or barriers that had remained hidden, usually surfaced once someone began working. When this happened, the support specialist had to go through the same barrier removal process used during the job search phase.

Since we couldn't test for alcoholism, for example, we often did not detect it prior to employment. Another example of a problem that surfaced after employment was inappropriate behavior, which took the form of insubordination, negativity, or being confrontational. Many times job seekers didn't display these behaviors in the workshop or during job search, but they came out on the job site.

Over the years we attempted to increase retention in several ways. The first was mentoring. Since child mentoring programs often provided the extra boost needed for some children's success, I hoped that the same would hold true for our members. We devoted much time and effort to designing our mentoring program. Dave approached some retired executives at our church about serving as mentors. They enthusiastically signed on. "Don't start loaning our folks money," he cautioned them. "Your job is to coach and encourage them."

Two of the men devoted a lot of time to mentoring some young, male members. One Saturday morning, our phone rang. "Dave, we've got a little problem," said Al, who had been CEO of a $10 billion business before retiring. "Charles is in jail."

"Don't bail him out, Al," said Dave. "What happened?"

"Well, it seems that Charles threw his wife out of the car and backed over her. She isn't dead, but she is sore."

Even the best-hearted mentors quickly got burned out due to a lack of basic understanding of the realities someone in poverty faced. In our culture we want to take Thanksgiving dinner to poor people and show our kids how generous we are. But when you are serving people who have struggled so much for so long, you may not see the same emotional return on investment that you get when giving dinner to a family. They may not hug you or smile at you or say "thank you."

We contacted many churches and were disappointed that few were willing to offer any mentors for adults. The volunteers we did get appeared uncomfortable with the members or came with preconceived ideas of proper behavior, which they felt they needed to teach. Others failed to keep proper boundaries and quickly became burned out. Some mentors were so unsure of themselves that they consumed too much of the staff's time with their questions and comments.

Another problem with mentoring was the lack of response from members. Frequently a member who agreed to commit to a mentoring relationship failed to show up for a mentoring session. The person who had agreed to be a mentor quickly lost interest. We detected an undercurrent of mistrust from our members when it came to mentors. Ruby Payne describes this classic disconnect between people in poverty and middle class as a failure to understand the "hidden rules," or unspoken cues and habits, of each economic class. Our middle class idea of a mentoring relationship didn't work for our members, and we discontinued the program.

A few years ago a faith-based organization called One City came to us and offered to establish a mentoring program for our members. Mentors from One City took ownership of the program and did not grow weary when some mentoring partnerships were unsuccessful. The One City mentor simply started over with another mentee. Even though this group hung in there for quite a while, eventually the partnership ended. The only truly successful mentoring program we have had was the Mentor Me program. We believe the reason this program was successful was because one staff person managed it on a full-time basis. She has since moved to another city, and we no longer have that program.

We also attempted to increase retention by holding alumni meetings one evening a month so members could share experiences and be recharged. At these meetings we served dinner, furnished babysitting, and offered a program that we thought would be helpful and of interest, but the meetings were very poorly attended. The folks who did attend were the ones who were already very committed to the program. Most of our members did not have energy left at the end of the day—at least not for a meeting that was going to reinforce job retention.

Another short-lived effort to improve retention was "Let's Talk," modeled on Alcoholics Anonymous. It was a meeting for members, run by members. The weekly brown bag lunch was established for the purpose of providing a means for those working and those looking for work to share their successes and problems and to get support and feedback from their fellow members. Our support specialist served as the moderator. If it had proven to be successful, we would have added a session in the evening to accommodate those who worked during the day, but the sessions were poorly attended. In many instances, they simply degenerated into a gripe session, and we quickly discontinued this effort.

Even though our retention rate remained far above average in comparison with similar programs, we were determined to raise it even higher. After many hours of meetings and discussing this issue, the team members came up with a plan that added some additional emphasis on retention. The "One Year at One Job" theme is mentioned at orientation, throughout the workshop and job search, and then again at the time of employment. Large signs throughout the office also serve to highlight this theme.

Every member who was employed got a copy of *The Retention Press,* a special newsletter that featured a story about someone celebrating a one-year anniversary at a job. It also mentioned all of those who had been on their jobs for three months, six months, and nine months. This newsletter gave tips for staying successfully employed and included a write-in advice column. The members loved it.

While the support specialist followed up with the member, the employment coordinator—the key contact person for employers—made contact with the employer. After a six-month period we saw encouraging results. The retention rate for core employers, one of the two retention rates measured, went from 48% to 56%. We learned that there was no one thing that would increase retention; instead we used a combination of strategies that kept our members focused on "One Year at One Job" one week at a time. We also discovered that what worked for one might not work at all for someone else.

As with job acquisition, pinpointing specific traits that led to long-term retention was difficult. But our research showed us that members who could cope with barriers and work through them, and those who had motivational strengths (for example, the desire to deal with a legal issue), were more likely to succeed.

"At the end of each month I look at the number of employments and retentions," said Darren. "I save messages that encourage me. One message I saved recently was from a member named Ben. He never said much in the workshop and always seemed to have a lot on his mind. He was a real responsible person, and for him not to have a job tore him up inside. Sometimes he'd come in to talk to me during job search, and he couldn't find the words. 'It's okay. You can just sit there as long as you need to,' I'd tell him. He finally landed a job with maintenance in the housing projects. I hardly recognized his voice when he called to tell me, he was so excited."

One afternoon after Ben had been on the job about three months, he came into the office. "I hope you aren't here because something happened on the job," said Darren, eyeing him warily.

Ben broke into a wide grin and said, "Oh, no, nothing like that. Everything is great with the job. I just came by on my break to say thanks."

The photographs of our members who reached their one-year anniversary with one employer covered the walls in our lobby. The numbers grew and grew until we started posting them all down the hallway. Their stories kept us going.

CHAPTER 11

Brother, Can You Spare a Dime?

"The greatest good you can do for another
is not just to share your riches,
but to reveal to him his own."
—Benjamin Disraeli

One of the most daunting tasks facing us on a continual basis was fund raising, especially since we were thankfully in a consistent growth mode. Nonprofits face myriad important decisions, and over the course of our history we've made some hard ones. For example, our decision over whether or not Cincinnati Works should become a member organization of our local United Way. In our early years we convinced United Way to fund us based on our performance. But we reached a point when the agency gave us the choice of becoming a full-fledged member organization or no longer receiving support. The dilemma was the same one we discussed in Chapter 1: If you accepted money through United Way, many funders who also donated to United Way considered it "double dipping" if you approached them directly for funding. Our board split on the vote; Beth and I cast the deciding votes, and we accepted continued United Way funding, which currently represents about 12% of our operating budget.

When you are fund raising, one of the most exciting things you can hear is that the funds you're receiving are unrestricted, meaning that your organization can use them however it needs to. Many funders only want to be involved in startups or have some other narrow focus. Early on Clay Mathile gave us his stamp of approval in the form of a three-year, unrestricted gift of $100,000 each year via the Mathile Family Foundation.

Dave met with Clay every year to discuss how we were doing and our plans for the future. "You use that money however you need to use it to meet your mission," said Clay, who, as the former owner and chair of The Iams Company, counted Dave as one of his closest business advisers. Over the next 15 years that gift continued to come our way. That sort of consistent support with the latitude to use it as needed gave us the foundation we needed to build Cincinnati Works. We were moved by the Mathiles' generosity and consistency. That sort of support is rare.

For a number of years we had attempted to obtain support from American Financial, an insurance and financial firm, and/or its creator, Carl Lindner Jr., without success. Then, a few years ago, one of our board members was able to obtain a $50,000 contribution payable in installments of $10,000 a year. This represented a real breakthrough for us since Carl Lindner Jr. was by far the most generous entrepreneur in our community.

When we returned from our 10th anniversary celebration, an envelope was lying in the middle of Dave's desk. In it was a substantial contribution from Mr. Lindner, along with a nice note regarding our decade of service to the community.

One of our members was employed by American Financial's maintenance department, and it was part of his job to clean Mr. Lindner's office. One day, as Mr. Lindner had a discussion with the man, it came up that the man was a Cincinnati Works member. When Mr. Lindner asked him about his experience with Cincinnati Works, he said, "It changed my life," and spent the next few minutes raving about us.

Given our growing relationship with American Financial and Mr. Lindner, Dave decided it might be good to visit with Mr. Lindner and explain more about what we were accomplishing and our future plans. He asked Dave Herche, a board member, to accompany him. They obtained an appointment with Mr. Lindner and his assistant for the purpose of explaining what Cincinnati Works was about and made it clear that this was not a funding call.

For about an hour they held a wide-ranging discussion about poverty. Dave told me later that it was the most informed conversation he had ever had with a business executive about poverty. As their visit came to a close, Mr. Lindner turned the meeting over to his assistant, who presented us with a $100,000 contribution—a $35,000 check and a pledge for the balance over the next two years. Dave and Dave were stunned at the outcome of the meeting. My husband Dave told me later that he did not know what to say—a rare occurrence —he was just caught so off guard.

The next morning Mr. Lindner's assistant called Dave and asked him if he and Dave Herche would join Mr. Lindner on a conference call that afternoon, which they scheduled. We couldn't imagine what Mr. Lindner wanted to discuss again so soon. I teased Dave that he probably wanted his contribution back.

Dave and Dave called at the scheduled time. Mr. Lindner explained that he had not realized the full scope of the accomplishments of Cincinnati Works. He wanted to double his contribution from the day before.

After this momentous telephone conversation, Dave and Dave went out to have a late lunch. Over lunch Dave Herche said, "After hearing that conversation, I don't think I've been doing enough for Cincinnati Works." That afternoon he wrote a check for $100,000 and continues to do so annually. I teased Dave that I'm waiting for him to top that 24-hour period when he raised more than a quarter of a million dollars.

When one of our funders and core employers turned down our funding request because of rules that put its contributions to organizations on a three-year rotating cycle, Dave boiled with frustration. He called Dave Herche, who as chairman of and majority owner of Enerfab, Inc., a metal fabricator more than a century old, happened to be a customer of that particular funder.

"We have to put people to work every year," Dave told Dave Herche, whom he had hired straight out of Miami University to work on his team at Arthur Andersen. "I happen to know that employer has hired 20 of our people in the last 14 months, and all 20 are still working for them."

"Well, why don't we pay a visit to the CEO and let him know that?" replied Dave Herche. "Maybe we can get an exception made."

The two men paid a visit to the company with records of the retention rates at the unskilled entry level. "Why don't you compare this retention rate to those entry-level employees you hired who didn't come from us?" my husband urged the CEO.

When the CEO compared the track record of Cincinnati Works members in the company's employ to that of other entry-level workers hired from other sources (who had a 50% turnover rate), he realized that we had saved the company almost $500,000 in retention costs in a few short years. Suddenly, the amount we were asking for in funding looked like a phenomenal investment. He agreed to give us permission to move ahead with our request for additional funding, and our request was approved.

We never put much stock in fund raisers—especially not splashy, black tie events. They were expensive and took a good deal of time and attention away from the business at hand, which was putting people to work. On top of that, Dave analyzed them and found that they rarely produced all that much in funding for the nonprofits that held them.

We concentrated on building relationships in the community for the long term. Some of the few events we did hold were intended to raise awareness. During one event called "Share the Learning," we presented research from studies we'd done. These events were open to the community and to the media.

In 2001 we adopted an idea from a doctor in Washington, DC, who served the homeless. We hosted a successful event called Womenade, a luncheon where we invited friends for a potluck lunch and suggested a donation of $35—about the cost of a night out on the town. We used the funds we raised for emergency utility assistance, prescriptions, eye exams and glasses, uniforms, food coupons, medical co-pays, and other items that helped our members through an unexpected barrier. The annual luncheon usually attracted almost 100 supporters, and year after year we raised about $3,000 for the direct assistance fund.

Lynn Marmer, a vice president at Kroger and a long-term funder, loved that event and had donated some food for it in the past. With our 10th anniversary fast approaching, Beth and I made an appointment with Lynn to ask her for a grant to underwrite part of the anniversary celebration.

"Absolutely not," Lynn said, and then she smiled. "We'll only be involved if you let us sponsor the whole thing."

Since our labor of love kicked off with Dave's surprise breakfast at the Banker's Club, we thought it fitting to celebrate a decade in operation with another morning meal. Katie Brown Blackburn, heir apparent to the Cincinnati Bengals and an attorney in charge of player acquisitions who also happened to have been one of my Sunday school students years ago, agreed to be our keynote speaker. The event was held at the Bengals' stadium.

The morning of our celebration, June 10, 2006, dawned bright and sunny. About 200 friends and fans of Cincinnati Works, along with our staff and many members, gathered at the stadium. We enjoyed breakfast courtesy of Kroger and then listened to a few speakers. A Cincinnati Bengals player agreed to come to the event, and he spoke about his own childhood in poverty. We seated him amidst our members. As one of our members spoke about his journey, I noticed his eyes well up.

Fund raising involves seeking, asking, finding, and yes, even a bit of begging. But when we saw our mission being realized every year in the lives of hundreds of families, we were not too proud to beg. We were able to collect much of our startup funding because of our relationships in the community. We didn't have any proof of our ability to reduce poverty in the beginning. After a decade of operation, contributions were made because of the real value Cincinnati Works added to our community. We proved that we could assist thousands of people in obtaining and retaining employment with the result of breaking the back of generational poverty.

We found that the annual letter we sent out during the holidays to friends and colleagues that we've met over the years proved effective at bringing in additional money. I always enjoyed writing that letter; it was like writing a fun family Christmas letter, only it was for our organization. Then, in 2006, I discovered that a picture was worth not only a thousand words, but thousands of dollars as well. I penned our usual holiday letter, but this time I highlighted the story of one of our members and put a picture in the letter. I'm not particularly tech savvy, and it had never occurred to me to do it before. This time the donations in response to the letter spiked, almost doubling from the previous year. Each year since then, the Cincinnati Works holiday letter has featured one member and told that person's story.

Over the years I became more and more focused on writing grants and working behind the scenes. As some of Dave's contacts retired, we realized we needed more help. There were also those firms that wouldn't support us directly because we were a United Way member organization. We hired Gale Parrish Sheldon to aid us in expanding our funding base. A widow who had been married to a highly successful attorney, Gale moved in social circles that we did not. She devoted herself to her work here and became a wonderful partner with me in our fund-raising efforts.

Procter & Gamble was an early supporter that helped get us started. They were one of five funders who made it possible for us to develop our "proof of concept": It was possible to move hundreds of people from poverty to self-sufficiency through work every year. Even though the initial funding we received from Procter & Gamble was incredibly helpful, we became ineligible for funding from them when we decided to continue receiving funding from United Way. Procter & Gamble would still continue to consider funding special projects, and we needed such funding to facilitate our move. We obtained an appointment with the staff. Dave came along, and we told them our story.

After the meeting we were told we could submit a request for this funding. Gale was enthusiastic and offered to help me, but I was disheartened because they wanted the request to be submitted online. Neither of us had much in the way of technology skills, and I felt there was no way to make your case in the few words the computer allows you. In my experience I'd be writing a main point and then the character limit would cut me off. But with Gale's help and some assistance from Tom Stilgenbauer, our chief financial officer, we were able to complete the application, and we awaited an answer, thinking the application had gone through.

Just to be sure, Tom followed up the next day to make sure Procter & Gamble had received the application, since the deadline was fast approaching. "Our system is clogged up and we're not sure," came the reply.

Two weeks later we got an email in response to the application that asked questions about our vendors and our banking relationships. Tom pitched in and helped me get the answers back to them quickly.

What had felt like a cold, passionless, and pointless exercise to me produced results beyond my wildest expectations. We were notified that we had been awarded a $100,000 grant from Procter & Gamble to fund our move.

We laughed. "I guess I know a development officer and a founder who need to improve their computer literacy," I said. "If you've got a good program, I suppose even a computer can figure that out."

Like all nonprofits, we competed for the available dollars in our community. Many worthwhile and necessary causes force potential contributors to make choices. Poverty was not what I'd call a "sexy" cause—one that generated lots of media attention and provided contributors and volunteers instantaneous feel-good feedback. At the end of the day you couldn't stand back and admire a house that you'd built or be rewarded by a sweet child's smile when you presented her with a toy at Christmas. Yet poverty was at the root of almost every ill we saw devastating the city we loved and fought for on a daily basis: drug abuse, alcoholism, mental and physical health issues, failure in school, and criminal activity, to name a few.

Moving a family from poverty to self-sufficiency generally required a minimum of 3–5 years and often took even longer. The painstaking process of coaching a person to approach work with a different mindset and equipping that person to be successful was full of setbacks and heartache. Nothing about it was simple. Nobody helping a person in poverty could reasonably expect instant gratification. Our staff understood and embraced the long-term dedication to coaching and to removing barriers that our members required. "We don't have the silver bullet to end poverty, but we have lots of silver BBs," Beth often said. "There's a lot of failure in this business. People come to us when they've been rejected and promises have been broken. Their hopes have been dashed. But this staff is just magical. You can't teach the kind of heart and compassion that they demonstrate.

"From a leader's standpoint, I look out for my staff. I work really hard to elevate my staff and give them permission to let it go at the end of the day. I tell them, 'This isn't your life or your failure if it doesn't work out for a job seeker.' When I worked in a cancer ward, I had to learn you can't change the fact that somebody has cancer, but you can be comforting and supportive. People come through our doors who are in so much pain. We see lots of people who have experienced sexual assault, domestic violence, abandonment, or who have alcoholic or drug-addicted parents. You can't change that, but you can be compassionate and help people find their resiliency. I've always thought that restoring hope is the best thing that we do."

We understood that burnout was one of the things we must guard against with our staff because we dealt with stressful situations on a daily basis. Our staff, which has an exceptionally low turnover rate, was vitally important to our continued success. The answer? We established an excellent employee assistance program and offered stress management classes. We also laughed a lot.

What our staff demonstrated in abundance was a deep capacity for providing a loving, warm, and supportive environment for our members. When potential funders came through on tours, they commented on that warmth, which often sparked them to take out their checkbooks. One funder, Norm Day, regularly contributed in order to "take care of the caregiver."

"You've got great people here," said Norm. "You can't risk burning them out."

Each year he gave an amount earmarked for something special for the staff. Some years we all went out to dinner. One year the staff got spa treatments.

The space we had rented was nondescript, a warren of offices with a few small classrooms carved out. The furniture, most of it donated or secondhand, wasn't anything special. Yet the spirit of kindness and exuberance of changed lives filled the place and welcomed people as soon as they arrived on our floor and were greeted by Gloria Hill, another of our members whom we hired as our customer service representative. The rich currency of being believed in flowed freely in our offices.

Poverty doesn't come cheap. The annual cost of existing government agencies serving a household in poverty was $30,000 a year in Cincinnati, which ranked within the top 10 poorest major cities in our nation. That cost to government agencies was repeated every year. We had worked and worked until our program got to the point where, for a one-time outlay of a little more than $2,500 we could put a person through our workshop and help that person get and retain a job. With the number of people we had helped obtain and retain jobs by the time our 10th anniversary rolled around, we had effectively saved the community well in excess of $100 million in services, and our members had earned millions of dollars in wages. Yet we were astonished that most communities demonstrated no sense of urgency about reducing poverty.

Nearly 30 years ago a toddler named Jessica fell into a well. It became a media event, with many folks across the country riveted by the drama unfolding before them. Before she was finally retrieved from that well, more than $10 million had been spent to rescue the girl. Everyone, including Dave and me, thought it was worth every penny to save her life. Yet, as communities and as a nation, we hesitate to rescue our endangered children from poverty at a mere fraction of what it cost to save Jessica.

More and more often when we inquired about the possibility of grants from foundations, we were told that we didn't meet the criteria because the foundation's only interest was in serving disadvantaged children. That baffled us. Children cannot be helped significantly in isolation from their families. There is a distinct relationship between family income and school success, according to a research study we commissioned from the University of Cincinnati Evaluation Services Center titled "Family Poverty: Its Implications for School Success." For example, during 2002–03, the 62.7% of Cincinnati public school students who were classified as economically disadvantaged scored below state proficiency levels at all grade levels in all subjects. Bill Shore, author of *Revolution of the Heart,* said, "You can't help a child without helping the child's parents."

Children elicited more sympathy than absentee fathers and mothers on welfare. Donors were far more attracted to programs that identified children as their beneficiaries. But to our thinking, this rationale was absurd: The 25% of children under age six who lived below the poverty line did not live alone. They were dependent upon their parents, grandparents, relatives, or caregivers and certainly could not thrive or even hope to do well if those taking care of them were mired in poverty.

Understandably, the "adopt a child for just $15 a month" type of solicitation holds great appeal, but no amount of direct aid to a young child, assuming it reached him or her (which again took a leap of faith), could succeed unless the child was in an environment where a caregiver—ideally a parent—nurtured, supported, taught, disciplined, and trained that child.

A friend's pediatrician always said that the best thing a man could do for a child was to love his or her mother. The best thing that society can do for disadvantaged children is to give their parents the support and services they need. In that sense, programs ranging from job training to adult literacy classes are social programs that help children.

Ironically, as our organization matured, we suffered from what I could only describe as a sophomore slump. We always set our budget goals based on our program goals *before* beginning the fund-raising process. Some nonprofits reverse this order, but we believed it was imperative to determine our needs first and then strive to raise the money to cover those needs.

We always maintained—or gave it our best effort to maintain—one or two years' operating expenses in reserve for three reasons: First, our staff's work was so fast-paced and demanding that we wanted them to focus on the mission and not worry about *their* next paychecks. Second, when a job seeker became a member, we made a commitment to be here for them until they reached self-sufficiency. Dave insisted that we be fiscally responsible so that we could fulfill that promise to every single Cincinnati Works member. Third, in the event that we encountered a poor year fund raising, the reserve would carry us through until the funding picked up.

With Dave's training as an auditor and accountant, he embedded best practices from the business world into our operation from the beginning. Ironically, our responsible stance backfired with some potential funders, who looked at our reserve and declined our funding request because they deemed other organizations struggling to meet the current payroll to be in greater need. Essentially, we were penalized for being financially responsible. Other funders liked the thrill of being involved with a startup, and we no longer qualified as an untested new kid on the block.

Cincinnati Works has always been run like a business, and we adhered to the following fiscal principles:

- Operate in a fiscally conservative manner with strong financial controls.
- Obtain operating funds at least a year in advance.
- Operate with a low fund-raising/administrative expense.
- Research unfilled needs of population served, build the business case, and raise the funds.

Research has been a hallmark of our nonprofit since its inception. We wanted to be certain we met the service needs of the poor by basing everything we did on facts. Too many nonprofits get caught up in chasing the money rather than sticking to what the real needs are and the original vision of the organization.

We have relied on the following process for fund raising:

Step 1: Study the characteristics of each major donor market.

Step 2: Organize your fund-raising operation (e.g., by donor markets, your services, marketing tools, geographic areas, etc.).

Step 3: Develop sound goals (incremental, need, or opportunity basis) and strategies (target markets and positioning) to guide the fund-raising efforts.

Step 4: Develop fund-raising tactics. How are you going to attack the market? Person-to-person calls, mail, phone, email?

Step 5: Evaluate fund-raising results (e.g., percentage of goal reached, expenses to contributions ratio, efficiency of development personnel).

Other challenges we faced in fund raising were funder fatigue, the desire of some funders to take time off (poverty doesn't take time off), the slowdown of the economy, local or national disasters that reallocated funders' resources, a lack of interest from foundations outside of our city, and the lack of multi-year commitments because of accounting requirements that forced contributors to present the gift in its entirety. Early on we lacked multi-year commitments, but as we started to stress this need, the Arthur Andersen alumni in our city stepped up. We held a reception for alumni at which they learned more about Cincinnati Works, and many of them made multi-year commitments.

We treated our funders as partners because without their investments, we could not exist. Besides sending the required Internal Revenue Service letter, we also sent a personalized thank you letter from the president, and in some cases a board member or one of our professionals also sent a thank you letter. All funders received our newsletter and annual report.

In addition, the Cincinnati Works president sent updates on progress and announcements of recognition. Each funder was encouraged to visit, take a tour, and ask questions. If anything, we wanted to over-communicate so that funders would be involved in our program throughout the year and understand how vital their investment was to the hundreds of families we touched each year as they began the process leading to self-sufficiency.

In the last few years we have worked hard to improve our social media presence. We have upgraded our website and are active on our Facebook, Twitter, LinkedIn, YouTube, and Google+ accounts.

Fund raising goes on year-round. The following schedule shows our fund-raising efforts:

Done before the start of the new year: Evaluate the previous year's fund-raising results to determine the new operating budget for the year. Based on the new budget, determine fund-raising gap. The annual fund-raising plan is developed and lays out in detail which funders we will approach in each category. Analyze our major donor markets, foundations, individuals, public grants, and events based on the previous year's fund-raising results. Target the specific donors to whom we will make requests for funding. Develop goals (expected amount to be received from each contributor) and strategies. Determine who will be contacted by whom and develop a timetable.

March to May: Begin to implement tactics. Conduct an "impact event" in April that highlights our previous year's impact on our community. Members speak about the impact of Cincinnati Works on their lives. Make one-on-one visits. Write grants. Target specific interests for funding to cover costs for our general job readiness program, Next Step program, and our Phoenix and advancement programs.

June to August: Continue visits and grant writing. Young Professionals group conducts a peer-to-peer social media campaign in July by sharing uplifting posts. Inspiring member stories are shared, and the solicitations are conducted by the group with help from our fund-raising staff. Each year the amount raised increases.

September: Follow up on requests.

October: Cincinnati Works is a United Way member and thus is not allowed to raise funds during United Way's fund-raising campaign. Request financial support of board of trustees. Our objective is to have 100% support from our board.

November: President conducts a letter-writing campaign. The founders also send letters to their friends.

December: We participate in the national fund-raising day, "Giving Tuesday," which takes place the first Tuesday in December. Final follow-ups and closeout of fund raising for the year.

Our funding comes from the following sources:
24% Individuals
24% Public Grants
23% Foundations
15% Corporations
10% United Way
4% In-Kind

Securing funding will always be frustrating and exhausting, but as one of our friends used to say, "You can't do the Lord's work without money." Somewhat to our amazement, Cincinnati Works thus far has raised more than $20 million for our fight against poverty. Everyone at Cincinnati Works worked hard to make the most of every dollar that came to us. Dave and I were truly humbled by the outpouring of our community.

The most precious donations to Dave and me were modest checks written by members. It reminded me of the poor widow Jesus commended for giving all she had to the temple collection. Our members' checks gave us a powerful vote of confidence. Those checks, often accompanied by handwritten thank you notes, meant that they had come full circle. They told us that everything we'd poured into this place had all been worth it.

CHAPTER 12

Outcomes: What Gets Measured Gets Done

*"Our life of poverty is as necessary as the
work itself. Only in heaven will we see how
much we owe to the poor for helping us to
love God better because of them."*

—Mother Teresa

"I see our number of workshop graduates for the last few
months was below what we projected," said Beth, our
president, in our noon staff meeting. "But we're doing above
our numbers on recruiting. Job retention looks good. Anybody
have any comments on these numbers?"

"We've seen a little dip in the number of employments with
our core employers too," said Everly, who had recently taken
over as the employment coordinator. "I think that reflects me
being new in the position."

A good portion of the next hour was taken up by a lively
discussion based around all the different numbers we tracked.
Any change in the numbers sparked examination of why this
condition existed and what we could do about it.

Spending so much time talking about numbers when you're
dealing with poor people's lives may seem cold at first. But we
made the numbers talk to us and translated them into action.
For example, when our number of employments flattened out

after three years, we hired a research company to explain the plateau. The numbers allowed us to correct faulty assumptions: We had assumed that if we matched the job seeker with the right employer, they would automatically advance; yet, the numbers told us that only 15% were advancing.

Not surprisingly, Dave, the accountant, constantly hammered home the need to measure outcomes. But none of us anticipated the difficulties we would encounter in trying to do so. Trying to measure the behavior of unpredictable adults in unstable circumstances was a challenge, to say the least. It was a little bit like trying to hold on to mercury at room temperature. The population we served moved frequently or sometimes simply vanished for a multitude of reasons. However, while keeping record of the people who had trusted us enough to invest their time to become members was certainly difficult and a big challenge, it was not impossible, as many agencies claimed.

What do we mean by *measurements* and *outcomes?* For our purposes, two simple definitions suffice. *Measurements* are the activities that are put in place to determine outcomes. They have evolved through the years. *Outcomes* are the results shown by the tools of measurement. They have remained constant since inception.

Being an outcome-based organization was vital to accomplishing the mission of Cincinnati Works. "The only measurements of success are job acquisition, long-term job retention, and self-sufficiency," Dave said.

Knowing the number of phone calls received, people attending the information sessions, people filling out an application, and people who started and completed the workshop was helpful, but if our members didn't go to work, they would not begin the vital process that led to self-sufficiency. And we always kept our eye on that all-important goal. Because we were outcome-based, we were diligent in reporting to our funders the total cost per placement based on all of the costs of the job readiness program plus allocated administrative and fund-raising costs. This level of reporting revealed fully loaded costs, which means that the cost of those not going to work was included with the cost of those who secured employment. Recording costs in this manner was unique in our industry. Tracking became an important process in order for us to accurately report our costs.

Measurements influenced the operation of our organization, and results were what we survived on. Before we made any decisions or took a new or different approach, we looked at what the numbers were telling us.

Based on the strategic plan, number goals are set each year for the following:

Job placements: They are recorded monthly under five headings:
1) Number of total employments
2) Number of new employments
3) Number of re-employments
4) Number of employments at core employers
5) Number of members placed

Job readiness numbers: In this report we record activities that lead to such desired outcomes as number of applications accepted, how many start the workshop, how many are in the job search, etc. In addition, such other information as job acquisition rate, job retention rate, total number working, and average hourly pay rate is included. Totals thus far are included each month. This report supplies bottom line information at a glance.

Retention report: This report records the percentage of those who have worked:
1) Three months at one job
2) Six months at one job
3) Twelve months at one job
4) Twelve months continuously, including those who have changed jobs

Self-Sufficiency: We track these data monthly based upon the actual wages of the members and use the most recent federal poverty guidelines as a basis to determine which members have achieved a living wage. We track wage gains as well, which tells us how many members start off earning a living wage and how many obtain it over time with wage increases. We also track how many members are above the federal poverty level to show incremental gains. Tracking people's journeys all the way from below poverty, to above the poverty line, and finally to self-sufficiency gives us a better overall insight into our members' progress.

Performance results report: These reports include such cumulative information as total number who:
- Have started the workshop
- Have been placed in a job for the first time
- Are currently working
- Have been employed for 12 months or more

In addition, these reports supply such employment data as the number of people who have gotten benefits with their job, those working at part-time jobs, and those working at jobs paying $9 or more per hour. Demographic data are also listed. Again, that information is often vital to our fund-raising efforts, because some funders have very specific groups that they want to help (working moms, for example).

Since 2009 Cincinnati Works has used Salesforce to track, monitor, and record all relevant data concerning our members and employers. The flexibility of Salesforce allows us to create and maintain a host of reports that track both members' and staff performance. We have created multiple custom dashboards and reports that give us timely updates on such metrics as applications, workshops, employments, and more. We can track monthly, year-to-year, and month-to-year data points as well. Salesforce also allows for ad hoc reporting as the need arises and allows us to track new data quickly, as well as remove old and irrelevant data. This allows us to respond quickly to both funding and outside agency needs. We use a combination of Salesforce and Excel for most of our reporting needs.

Measurements continue to influence the operation of our organization. The most significant decision we made based on the numbers was when we added advancement to our program. When we noted that members were not achieving self-sufficiency on their own, even though it was possible with their employers, we knew we had to add a process that would help them move toward that goal.

Over the years we have used our reporting system to guide our efforts in many other areas as well, including:

1) Marketing. Choices are constantly being made based on the number of people responding to a particular effort—for example, an ad in a newspaper or a public service announcement on television.

2) When too many people were stuck in the job search because of police records, we decided we needed to expand the employer base to include more employers that would hire people with a past record.

3) After looking at retention numbers, we knew we needed to add processes that would increase retention.

4) When we noted that we had only a 50% attendance rate on the first day of the workshop among those who had been accepted into Cincinnati Works, we researched the problem and added reminder phone calls and postcards to the process. We also adjusted our screening process to attempt to improve the show rate.

5) We became alarmed when too many members were quitting or being terminated from our core employers. That's when we developed an infraction policy for members working for core employers.

These examples illustrate that compiling and analyzing numbers, which constantly guides us in our decision making, is one of the main reasons for the successes we have had. Even though measuring real outcomes is difficult and not completely precise, it is close enough to keep us focused on the mission. A common pitfall for nonprofits that do track numbers is becoming obsessed with perfection, which can end up wasting time and money. "Close enough is okay as long as we get directional trends," Dave often reminded our staff.

Not only do we have extensive performance outcomes, we place a similar emphasis on financial outcomes as well. Our key financial reports are summarized below:

Annual budget: The budget is prepared based on our estimate of what it will cost to achieve our projected performance outcomes. After approval by the board, the budget is broken down on a monthly basis.

Monthly financial statements: These are prepared within 10 days of month's end. The actual monthly and year-to-date results of operations are compared to the budget, and differences are analyzed so appropriate corrective action can be taken. This analysis helps us make timely changes so that we can stay on course.

Revenue analysis: The purpose of this analysis is to identify all of our funders since inception. This tool has proven very useful in helping us plan our annual fund-raising goals and notice immediately any changes in funders' level of giving. This information is critical in preparing our annual fund-raising strategy and goals.

Annual report: Included in this report are the yearly audited financial statements. Our annual report highlights a different theme each year so that investors can be made aware of program activities. It also offers another opportunity to emphasize that everything we do is about the people in poverty we serve. It is also used in our awareness tool to assist the reader in understanding that there are practical solutions to poverty.

Business case: Our overall business case is revisited every three years or so. It is extremely helpful in assisting us to think through what our operations and results of operations will look like 3–5 years out. Then we can plan our activities and future direction more efficiently.

When we approach a potential funder, we are able to demonstrate that we are outcome-based, both in program and financial results.

Keeping detailed records about where our people went to work and how long they stayed there paid off. In fact, proof that we were able to save companies a fortune in hiring and retention costs led to our process being written up in a *Harvard Business Review* article titled "Tapping a Risky Labor Pool" in December 2006.

Two professors at Miami University, Brian Ballou and Dan Heitger, had become familiar with our work and were excited about the original, research-driven model that we'd developed. They set out to get a case study on us published. In their study, called *An Innovative Approach to Workforce Retention,* Ballou and Heitger noted that we obtain results for both the chronically unemployed and the companies that hire them— companies like Fifth Third Bank, Citigroup, Greyhound, and HMS Host, to name a few. When the professors—along with Dave, who patiently answered several rounds of questions from the *Harvard Business Review* editor—finally worked their way through the exhaustive 18-month process and got their article published, the editors told them that theirs was one of a very small number of articles published in the *Harvard Business Review* without having been generated or commissioned by the staff. The other thing that made our inclusion in the *Harvard Business Review* such a coup was that the magazine has very rarely published articles about nonprofit organizations.

In the final article that ran in the *Harvard Business Review,* the authors focused on Fifth Third Bank, where 90% of workers hired through Cincinnati Works have stayed at the company at least a year, nearly twice the company's average retention rate of 50% for employees in comparable jobs.

Why the sharp contrast in retention? As Ballou and Heitger explained, industries that rely heavily on unskilled workers must draw from a labor pool made up of those who are chronically unemployed or are considered to be working poor because they earn less than 200% of the federal poverty level. Many of these people face barriers to employment success that go beyond their unstable work history: behavioral issues, poor communication skills, and the like. Through our unique, comprehensive approach, we systematically work with our members to reduce these barriers.

The article described how, in addition to providing help in job training, placement, retention, and advancement, Cincinnati Works also offered members a lifetime of wrap-around services—everything from legal, mental health, and spiritual counseling to emergency relief for basic needs.

"We're thrilled about this national seal of approval," Beth told our board at the first meeting after the article came out. "It's more validation that Cincinnati Works works. And not just for our members, but also for the core employers we work with. The authors really homed in on that fact, providing hard numbers on how we have reduced turnover and, as a result, saved local companies hundreds of thousands of dollars."

About a third of our funding came from the local business community, and Dave's focus on numbers had earned us respect from business leaders. Getting that validation in a quality national publication provided the evidence that poverty can be dealt with in a cost-effective, efficient manner.

CHAPTER 13

Progress

*"I know the price of success: dedication,
hard work, and an unremitting devotion
to the things you want to see happen."*
—Frank Lloyd Wright

The cowbell clanged loudly. Word spread quickly throughout our office. Jack had just landed his dream job. Well, almost. The 45-year-old got the call that told him he nailed his interview with Norwegian Cruise Lines. Although there wasn't an opening for a cook, which was what he had trained for, he agreed to take a job as a galley steward since the cruise line offered in-house job posting. As soon as he got word, he immediately called Nicole Ware, our director of community relations, to share his good news.

When Jack came to us, he was on the verge of losing his apartment. Nicole, who was doing intake that day, told him he didn't fit the criteria since all members must have a stable place to live.

"Please, let me get my mama on the phone," Jack begged. "She'll vouch for me and pay my rent for the next few months. I know I can do this."

Nicole relented and let Jack make the long distance call to his mom in Dayton.

Jack made good on his promise and was the first one through the doors for the workshop every day. We helped him learn how to interview. He took a 10-week cook's course and invited us all to his graduation from Cincinnati Cooks. Two days before his graduation, he landed a job. In his speech he tearfully thanked the Cincinnati Works team—"especially Nicole."

That first job he got was cooking for homeless children at Cincinnati Union Bethel, the oldest social service agency west of the Allegheny Mountains. "I ain't missed a day yet; in fact, I'm always early," he said. His good work ethic won him a promotion to head cook with the responsibility of planning the menu and budgeting for three meals a day. He kept that job for more than a year, but always in the recesses of his mind Jack dreamed of traveling. He'd never been out of the United States and had been on an airplane only twice, but he couldn't get it out of his mind.

When he heard about the job fair and the cruise ship opportunity, he called his employment support specialist to help him polish his resume. He put on his best suit for the interview.

After he got the job, he rushed over during the break in his split shift at the shelter to fill out some paperwork and thank Nicole in person. "I'll get four squares a day, uniforms, and my room," he said. "The only thing I've got to pay for are toiletries. I'll be gone 10 months out of the year."

We asked him what he planned to do about his apartment. He paused and then said softly, "I'm keeping my apartment for now. I'm proud of myself for keeping it for seven years. I'm not ready to let that go just yet."

In the fall of the year of our 10th anniversary, we hosted another "Share the Learning" event. This one had the theme "Why Don't They Just Get a Job?" More than 50 people attended the forum, which highlighted our decade of learning and research centered on the misconceptions surrounding this question and the real issues behind chronic unemployment. The panel of presenters included our mental health counselor, chaplain, legal advocate, and employment support specialists.

"Many of us working to eliminate poverty too often hear this old question, as though the only thing the chronically unemployed lack is the will to work," Beth told the audience gathered at the downtown branch of the Cincinnati Public Library. "That is simply not the case. Our members face a variety of barriers ranging from a lack of skills and knowledge regarding applications and interviewing to anxiety and depression. Cincinnati Works has learned what it takes to help our members knock down these barriers."

When Dave and I started Cincinnati Works, we focused on our own backyard and didn't allow our thoughts to go much beyond that. Since our first few encounters with the media had left us feeling misunderstood and treated with suspicion, we had never sought attention. Besides, with such a lean organization, none of us had any time to publicize what we were doing that was so different from all the other workforce development efforts out there.

However, after a decade in operation, we began to get more and more local and national recognition, and Dave and I both realized that through our constant questioning of the process and looking for better and better ways to help the poor obtain self-sufficiency, we'd discovered a brand new model with efficient results that systematically and substantially reduced poverty. What we did here day after day was about so much more than just getting a job. It was about changing a life by assisting our members as they fought to eliminate their barriers to employment. Sixty-two percent of our members have dependent children. If you help the parent, you are helping the child break the cycle of poverty.

After we were recognized by the American Institute for Full Employment as the best in the nation for our best practices, several members of our board encouraged us to explore ways to expand the concept to other communities. We began to dream of broadening our reach and touching the lives of many, many more families beyond Greater Cincinnati.

In short order we won several other honors in 2007, including an Impact 100 grant and the ONE Award, which recognizes nonprofit organizations for best practices. We were also included in the top 10 finalists in the U.S. in 2007 for the Manhattan Institute Social Entrepreneurship Award, and in 2009 we were a winner.

The time had come to tell our story and the stories of the members of Cincinnati Works.

Beth was working in her office around 3 p.m. when Anthony Carson from Class #9 entered to empty the trash. "You know, Beth, I just celebrated my seventh year here at Cincinnati Works in January," he said. "Thought you might like to know that my daughter Ariel is getting recruited by all kinds of colleges. Next weekend we're going to visit the University of North Carolina. She wants to be a doctor. You know, I had to learn how to waltz because she was a debutante. Imagine that."

"That's great, Anthony," Beth said. "How is your son doing?"

"He's got a mouth on him, but I guess that's okay because he wants to be a lawyer or a preacher," Anthony replied. "He's got a 3.6 GPA. I've got both of them working part-time busing tables over at the Millennium Hotel. It's a union job at $7.40 an hour. And it's nice they work where I work."

"Wow, that's fantastic. You and your wife are doing a great job with those kids."

In 2007 Anthony was still working for the Millennium Hotel on the night shift making $14 an hour and had been named employee of the month five times. "I tell my son, 'You don't have to be the employee, you can be the employer,'" Anthony said. "Opportunity is there knocking at the door. All you got to do is open it."

Then he paused and said, "Beth, I want to thank you again. I've got nice money saved up, and I'm not in debt. I'm happy. The Lord has blessed us."

Rex, 45, came in to see Jodie to discuss his effort to gain custody of his 10-year-old daughter. "Hey, Ms. Jodie," he called cheerily.

He had been employed with Brantley Security Services for 11 months. When Rex came to us, he had temporary housing at Tender Mercies, but his time at the shelter was running out. Because of our rule that a job seeker must have stable housing so potential employers can reach them, the church gave Rex an extension so he could attend our workshop. A priest there sensed that Rex was sincerely trying to get his life together.

After high school Rex joined the U.S. Army and became a Chinook helicopter mechanic. After three years in the military he was honorably discharged. Eventually he signed up for an apprenticeship program, earned his journeyman's card, and worked as a commercial roofer for more than a decade.

In the summer of 2005 he was working on a roof when he got dizzy and slipped off the asphalt. At the veterans hospital he was diagnosed with high blood pressure and told to avoid prolonged exposure to heat and sunlight—not an easy order for a roofer. The next day he worked 11 hours, but, "I felt like Babe Ruth in his last year of baseball. I knew I'd played my last game. I went to my boss and said, 'I'm done.'"

He'd been divorced for two years at that point. He stayed for a time with a nephew and cousin and tried to start a landscaping business, but that never got off the ground. Things went from bad to worse. He finally got a part-time job making sandwiches at Subway, but his brother told him the gasoline that it took to get him to his $6.25 an hour job wasn't worth the trouble. His car was repossessed, and he began suffering anxiety attacks.

Eventually Rex ran out of relatives to stay with. A church gave him a referral to Hamilton County Jobs and Family Services. "They said because I didn't have any drug or alcohol issues, they couldn't refer me to a shelter," recalled Rex, a deeply religious man. He stumbled upon the St. Francis/St. Joseph Catholic Worker House around the corner from a Walmart where he applied for work.

"They told me they didn't have any beds that night, but they let me spend the night in the drop-in shelter," said Rex. "I used my bag as a pillow and kept my shoes on, because I didn't want to take a chance on them not being there the next morning. And I asked them to lock up my medication."

The next day a permanent bed opened up, and the priest remembered Rex. "With my last money I got a bus to go pick up my paycheck from Subway," he said. "The house was closed from 9 a.m. to 4 p.m., so that meant I needed to go look for a job. They told me about Cincinnati Works, and I figured I didn't have anything to lose."

His eyes lit up when he talked about meeting Jodie and how she'd given him courage in the struggle to gain custody of his daughter, who was with Child Protective Services in another state. "Sometimes you meet a person at the right place, right time," he said.

Jodie recommended him for the job in security with Brantley. Part of Rex's plan to reunite with his daughter required him to take parenting classes. But he also needed a job to provide him stability. "Take the job, Rex," Jodie told him. "I'll work on finding a parenting course that fits your schedule." He started the classes in January 2006. The staff at the Catholic Worker House nominated him for a partnership that helped him get a one-bedroom apartment.

The next hump to overcome was getting a two-bedroom apartment—one of the state's requirements for him to get his daughter out of foster care. "Goodwill paid my deposit and first three months on the condition that I pay outstanding debts equal to the rent," he said.

When he applied for a two-bedroom, Metropolitan Housing denied his application because his child wasn't in his physical custody—a typical government catch-22 that we try help our members navigate.

"When you remain obedient and keep your trust in the Lord, you'll receive blessings you can't count," said Rex. "After three years of living with other people, in my car, and then in a shelter, it sure is nice to open up my door and say to myself, 'Welcome home.'"

Around the time of our 10th anniversary celebration, the numbers we were serving began to outstrip the capacity of our employment support specialists. I believed it had something to do with our new recruiter, Linda Humphries.

At the information session, Linda, a soft-spoken woman, opened her presentation by telling those attending that she was a Cincinnati Works member. After the department store where she worked for 27 years was acquired by a new company, Linda found herself out of work for 18 months.

"I didn't think it was going to be that difficult to find a job," she said. Then her mom got sick and moved in with her. "I was depressed and in a crunch situation. I was in survival mode."

Finally she got a third-shift casual labor job as a mail handler with the post office, but she had no benefits for 18 months. Jodie was impressed with Linda and remembered her when a customer service representative position opened up in July 2005.

"I was afraid of the position," she told her audience. "I felt nervous about my computer skills, and my confidence had been shaken to the core. I've walked the same walk you might be walking now."

Eventually we promoted Linda to recruiter, where she has thrived. "I never knew I'd find a family when I started working here," said Linda. When Sister Jeanne retired, Linda took on her chaplain duties as well.

The team we eventually assembled at Cincinnati Works came from as diverse a range of backgrounds as the people we served. The commonality was a deep desire to make a difference in the lives of everyone who walked through our doors. And we did become a family in a sense.

Carol Buschhaus, who had a degree in business and another in marketing, had spent 20 years teaching high school marketing before she took a part-time job with us in development. She hadn't been with us long before we enlisted her to be a support specialist.

"I now have 65 in the job search, 175 in retention, and my voicemail stays full," said Carol. "I never dreamed I'd be doing this job, but I love it."

She displayed a sensitivity and warmth our members responded to. One day she noticed a Native American man in his late 40s, his hair in a long ponytail down his back, struggling to fill out an application. He had an eighth-grade education and had scarcely been out of Northern Kentucky. He had gotten a job interview but shyly told her that he wasn't going to go. She was intuitive enough to realize he was afraid of getting lost on his way to the interview because his reading skills were so poor.

"I'll go with you on the interview," she volunteered. She accompanied him on the bus route so that he'd know the way if he did get hired.

Carol is still with Cincinnati Works and has become our workshop facilitator. The man in the story?

He got the job.

In our constant effort to look for ways to help people become self-sufficient, and after discussing some of the cases we had encountered, we decided to offer Jacque's mental health counseling services to people who hadn't been through our program but who were struggling with advancement.

Ralph, a man in his early 40s, started working in a bedding warehouse right after high school graduation making $12 an hour. He grew up in the Winton Terrace projects in Cincinnati with a single mom and two brothers. The $12 an hour he earned at the warehouse seemed like a fortune to him. He stayed at that job for 11 years until the company was acquired by another firm and he was laid off.

"I had deep, deep self-esteem problems," he said. "I heard about Cincinnati Works through a mutual friend."

After starting in the stockroom at T. J. Maxx, he was on his way to management after seven years with the company, but Ralph kept derailing himself when he came up for a promotion. "That's why I came to see Jacque," he said. "Negative thinking can really do a number on your life. And in this society, being a black male is twice as hard. You always think you're not good enough."

The first time he was offered a managerial post, he turned it down. He was passed over for the next opening. He worked up his courage to ask about the position and was told his manager wasn't sure he could be trusted with a store because he'd been so negative about the promotion the first time it was offered. Jacque worked with him to help him control his anxiety and redirect his thinking.

"The truth was I was scared. I didn't believe I could get it," he said. "I was afraid to transfer to another environment because I was terrified I wouldn't be successful. Those sessions with Jacque helped, and my district manager gave me another chance. Now I'm three months into my new promotion and everything is going fine."

Our members' paths to success rarely followed a straight, upward trajectory. At times progress seemed almost imperceptible, but slowly, each and every day, lives were being transformed. Some transformations I would call small miracles, but miracles nonetheless. I looked forward to coming to work every day to see what new miracle the day would bring forth.

CHAPTER 14

New Challenges

"Constant kindness can accomplish much.
As the sun makes ice melt, kindness
causes misunderstanding, mistrust,
and hostility to evaporate."
–Albert Schweitzer

Our weekly staff meetings at noon on Mondays were never boring. We applauded successes like a large, unexpected donation from an unlikely source. We lamented a member losing his job—again. In the short time we had been working with the chronically unemployed, our accomplishments far exceeded our initial dreams for the organization.

In June 2007 our staff meeting agenda was different. We had been approached by several organizations to develop the employment piece for a radical new program inspired by a program in Boston known as the "Boston Miracle," which was aimed at getting gang members to trade in their guns and stop the violence. It would be a departure from the way we had operated over the past 11 years, and I was concerned about the strain it would put on our already busy staff.

We got right to the issues.

"What would this mean for the people we turn down because they don't pass the drug test?" asked Linda, who handled intake and drug testing.

"That's a really good question," said Beth. "I'm not sure we're going to get all the answers today, but let's just get everything out on the table."

"What kind of numbers do we think this will bring?" asked Jacque.

"Well, the experts who worked with the program in Boston aren't expecting that many to go for employment, but that wasn't offered as part of the deal in Boston," Beth replied.

For the next hour we debated whether we had the capacity to handle the request and whether it would in any way harm the progress we'd worked so hard for. Would our city's most violent criminals give up their often deadly turf wars and drug dealing in exchange for earning their own way, supporting their families, and staying out of jail?

Despite the daunting challenges, the staff decided to move ahead and participate with the Cincinnati Initiative to Reduce Violence (CIRV) program. We developed some rough guidelines that day and hammered out the details and methodology for the key components in subsequent meetings.

On July 31, 2007, a local judge summoned 75 of the city's most notorious gang members to his courtroom. Fifty showed up. He told the group that they were being offered an alternative to their violent lifestyles.

Law enforcement officer Michael Blass attended the first call-in. He described the gathering of hardened criminals, criminal justice professionals, social service providers, and community members: "The young men were used to being in control; now they were off balance."

He observed in astonishment as Dr. Victor Garcia, a surgeon at Children's Hospital, a product of affirmative action, and a friend of Dr. C. Edward Koop, talked to the young men sitting before him. Dr. Garcia was raised in Harlem, but while his friends succumbed to the lure of the streets, he excelled at Jesuit schools and West Point. He pointed out that black men killing black men could potentially destroy the black race.

He looked straight at the men and said, "I love you, and God loves you. You've got to want more than this for yourself." The room went silent.

Dr. David Kennedy of the Boston Miracle spoke at the gathering as well. Kennedy also worked with gang members and has called Dr. Garcia "Mother Teresa in a man's body." He told the group that when Boston began prosecuting gang members to the full limits of the law, gun violence went down 40% the first year and 70% the second.

In Cincinnati the rules laid out that day were equally strict. One of the law enforcement officials told the men gathered in the courtroom, "If you have a gun on you without a permit, you can be put in prison for 15 years. A bullet in your pocket will get you eight."

The mother of a young man who had been killed in a gun battle evoked strong emotions from the gang members. She talked of her anguish and her anger at losing her son, but she reiterated Dr. Garcia's words, saying, "I love you too."

As Beth looked around the courtroom, she saw a few of the men wipe tears from their eyes, their faces visibly softened. "Many of them just looked tired," she said.

Michael Blass was astonished that a few openly admitted wanting to change. Not one tried to justify the violence. "This is profound change," he said.

Some of those involved with what was dubbed the Boston Miracle had confided in Beth that we'd likely only get a few leads from that first call-in. Over the next month we were astonished when 44 men called the special hotline number on the Cincinnati Works cards handed out at the meeting, 25 who had been in the courtroom that day and the rest by word of mouth.

We developed an employment service delivery process. The initial contacts for individuals seeking CIRV services were to come through either Stan Ross, director of the city-employed street advocates, or our mental health staff person, Jacque Edmerson. Oymma Barker served as the employment support specialist for anyone who came through CIRV. Jessica Dunham, the coordinator of the law enforcement team, worked in concert with the group.

The process began when a street advocate—a city employee who worked on the streets and was accessible via cell phone 24/7—accompanied each gang member to our office, where he was assessed by Jacque. Successful candidates were required to attend our 30-hour job readiness workshop that started every Monday. We briefly considered pulling them out separately for their own workshop, but realized that they were simply job seekers too.

We decided to offer a support group on Thursday afternoons, recognizing that the men in the CIRV program were dealing with radical shifts in their lives. Beth brought in a homemade meal and was touched when she was asked if she'd like to stay. "I started looking forward to Thursdays," she said. "The men were so open. Several told me that coming here to Cincinnati Works was the first time in their lives that they'd ever felt hope. One young man in his early 20s said,

'I come here and I feel like somebody cares whether I live or die.'"

Without a program like this, the statistics were grim. If men and women were not steadily employed by the time they reached 30, the likelihood was that they would never attain self-sufficiency. Instead of discouraging us, that statistic only served to intensify our determination to do our part to make CIRV a success.

Results to date have surpassed our wildest expectations. By April 2009, 390 men and a few women had contacted CIRV for services. Of that number, 352 (90.3%) completed an intake assessment and an individual life goal change plan with Jacque. She assigned 306 to the job readiness workshop (86.9%), and 221 (62.8%) started the workshop. Of that number, 153 (43.5%) completed the workshop, and all 153 started the job search. One hundred of those job seekers (28.4%) obtained a job, and 53 (15.1%) were employed.

"We've been so encouraged by the determination of those participating in CIRV," said Oymma, whom we promoted to director of career development and who continued to serve as the support specialist for those in CIRV while overseeing the other support specialists.

Many CIRV program members talked freely about their experiences. One said sadly that a friend he had known since they were three years old turned on him. "You have to be friendly to crackheads because that's where your money is coming from, and the crackheads are the ones who could turn you in," he said angrily.

We tried to encourage and support them in all the changes they were facing. What surprised us all was the level of weariness and deep desire to change. Part of the process involved explaining that they can't be part-time on the street and part-time legitimate. They had to make a wholesale change. When we asked them what their values were, not one talked about getting a job. Many said taking care of their family but failed to make the connection between the two.

Many street advocates came from the same communities and had walked in these shoes. Mitch, a team leader, was locked up a few times, but he put that life aside when he wound up with full custody of his son, who had dyslexia and learning disabilities. "Here I am, a gangster from the streets," he told us. "How was I going to get him the help he needed?" Mitch devoted his life to getting straight and getting help for his son, working janitorial and odd jobs so that his son could attend a private school. He was ineligible for most better paying jobs.

Mitch could scarcely believe how his life turned around. As a convicted felon he never dreamed he could work for the City of Cincinnati or that he would sit in on high-level meetings and participate in events at City Hall.

"God moved mountains," he said. "For the first time in my life I've got benefits. I've even got health insurance."

Mitch's job as a street advocate began when one of his mentors brought an application to his house. It happened to be the day Mitch had wrapped up his brainchild: the Safe Summer Celebration program, which touted the Stop Guns in the Streets campaign. His modest house was filled with posters and balloons and pamphlets on all kinds of health issues. He had started putting on the event on his own a few years ago, and it had grown in popularity.

"He seen how it was with me," Mitch said of his mentor. "He didn't give up on me. I'd been turned down so much, I didn't want to waste my time. He said, 'Just fill it out, and I'll take it for you.' It was the last day they were taking applications.

"The happiest I have ever been is at CIRV," he said. "I found out that purpose I had in my chest the whole time was the heart God gave me. I just didn't know how to use it. Cincinnati Works makes you feel like somebody, especially if you've got kids." He called Cincinnati Works and the Cincinnati Police Department like being on a "dream team."

Mitch, whose son now attends college, had about 20 people in his caseload and provided transportation to support meetings for up to 15 of them. Mitch told us he was thrilled to be considered one of the mentors instead of the one needing the mentoring.

"Some of the guys feel they have had a foot on their neck for so long, they stopped believing," he said. "I tell them, 'Success is in your future.'"

After several years the city no longer had funding for many of the CIRV services, and Mitch was laid off. But as a volunteer he continued to bring us potential candidates for what we now call the Phoenix program. The purpose of this program continues to be assisting willing people to leave a criminal life on the streets and become productive through work. We were gratified to find that there are employers ready to hire graduates of Cincinnati Works, even if they are ex-offenders. Many times those employers are people who were in a similar predicament at one point. When they decided to turn their lives around, they couldn't find employment and ended up starting their own businesses.

Mitch has developed a relationship with the police, and they now call him as soon they get a call that a homicide has been committed. He is on call 24/7 to go to the homicide scene, comfort the victim's family, and try to prevent retaliation. He works with some of those he meets and tries to convince them that there is a better way to live their lives. If they are ready to make a change, he mentors them and gets them ready to start the Phoenix program. Since the Phoenix program's inception, 426 people have gotten jobs, and the retention rate of nearly 80% is higher than our other programs.

Because Mitch wasn't getting much sleep, we told him to hire some help! He found four other men who work part-time, and lately we have seen the Phoenix staff on the local news being interviewed at crime scenes. Unfortunately, as crime becomes more prevalent in our city, there is more need for the work of Mitch and his team.

Princess Malik spent five years in prison for drug trafficking. During that time her sister and brother-in-law took care of her three children, ages 11, 6, and 10 months. After Princess Malik was released, she needed to fill out a mountain of paperwork to get her children back. The Phoenix program helped her with that. After she attended the workshop, we helped her get a job as a cashier at a restaurant. She has done well there, now has an apartment, and her three children are living with her again.

Foster kids aging out of the system at 18 are the very definition of the term "throwaway kids." They have often been physically, sexually, or emotionally abused at home, attended multiple schools, and been shuttled from foster home to foster home. Most are 2–3 years behind academically, and a startlingly large percentage of foster kids aged 16–18 drop out of school every year. Few adults have remained steadfast in their lives. And because the Hamilton County Department of Jobs and Family Services is facing financial constraints and must increase funds for overburdened juvenile courts, there is enormous pressure to get the kids out of the system the day they turn 18.

Placement opportunities dwindle as the children get older, and this is compounded by behavioral disorders, mild developmental disabilities, and delinquent behaviors. But even well-behaved foster children face terrible odds. For every 1,000 kids there are 10 foster parents, and the tougher the kid, the more placements they have endured. In addition, caseworkers come and go, sending mixed messages. Some foster homes are even rife with abuse. Group homes are often worse. Smaller, more vulnerable teens are harassed and beaten up by other kids. They have been neglected for so long that they are frustrated and angry. At the Cincinnati center known for housing tough kids, 63 are felony offenders, and 45 have completed their GEDs. Only 3–5 graduate every year.

Nationally, 30,000 adolescents age out of the foster care system each year. Their future is bleak unless we come up with viable solutions. The Child Welfare League of America reports that as many as 36% become homeless, 56% become unemployed, and 27% of males are jailed. According to *The San Francisco Chronicle,* less than half have graduated from high school, compared with 85% of all 18- to 24-year-olds. Fewer than one in eight graduate from a four-year college, and two thirds have not maintained employment for a year. Forty percent of the males become parents.

To help emancipated foster youth find employment and their way to self-sufficiency, we embarked upon an 18-month pilot program called Next Step, available to those aged 17½ to 25 who had been in foster care or the juvenile justice system. Working in concert with Lighthouse Youth Services, ProKids, the Children's Home, the Department of Jobs and

Family Services, and Leadership Cincinnati, we tried to figure out how best to meet the needs of this unique population as they went through our job readiness, job retention, job search, advancement, and management of barriers programs.

One of the challenges we battled was that many of the kids were so tired of being in the system that the last thing they wanted to do was sign up to be involved with another organization. Establishing trust remains a big issue.

Even though it is difficult to work with kids in this program, the pilot turned into a regular program, and an organization called Impact 100 continued to fund it. Since then, other funders have joined to help keep this program going.

Currently there are 29 former foster kids in the program, 18 have obtained jobs, and there are two in our advancement program. Dave and I feel this program is essential. We can't throw kids away. Just like with the chronically unemployed, the biggest challenge is figuring out how to motivate former foster youth to stay in a job and become independent workers.

Sue, 25, was a middle child of eight siblings. She spent a chunk of her childhood, from ages 6–12, in foster care. For six months she worked at The Limited Too at Kenwood Towne Center for $7 an hour before being laid off. "They just stopped giving me hours," she said.

"I was on my own for two years until I ran into Ms. Linda at the Fourth Street Boutique," said Sue. "She told me about Cincinnati Works, and I went through their workshop.

"Now I tell other foster kids about Next Step. They are just drawn to me, even those that seem to have a bad attitude at first. Then they tell me their story. It's usually the same: The system gave them back to their mother, but she was still messed up. No wonder they have a bad attitude."

To get by she collects food stamps and lives in subsidized housing, where she has one room and a kitchen. "In four or five years, if I stayed in the old pattern, I'd still be getting by on $90 worth of food stamps—less than $3 per meal. Some days I don't eat anything all day but a bag of potato chips. But what am I gonna do?"

Sue also had a 13-year-old niece in foster care in a group home in Toledo. "I want to be a model, a gospel singer, or write books," she said wistfully. "I want to earn enough money to get my niece out of there.

"At first I despised being at Cincinnati Works; I thought they were trying to trick people in some kind of way. They gave us group assignments and beat us up about what we didn't do right. They kept telling us stuff that I already knew.

"By the second day that changed. Cincinnati Works was helping me understand the business world. I couldn't believe I was face to face with businesspeople. I thought people believed they were better than us. At Cincinnati Works they are actually taking time to tell us secrets of how you get a job—how employers are thinking.

"My support specialist tells me what I need to do to uplift myself and not to sell myself short. They tell me what to say to employers. I learned more than just how to get a job. In a crazy way, it teaches you how to live life, how to think positively, and how to attract people from the outside world. They also taught me how to break away from people who aren't good for me. The people at Cincinnati Works seen something in me. Just because you came from poverty, you don't have to become that. I feel like I'm getting into alignment now and stepping into who I am even though my environment keeps trying to pull me back down. I want to be the next Oprah and have Mr. Dave and Ms. Liane on my show."

In 1995, when we were doing research to see if there was a need for Cincinnati Works based on the number of people living in poverty in our community, we noticed that there were five pockets of poverty in the Greater Cincinnati area. We realized that we would be more effective if we could eventually establish satellite offices in those areas.

In 2012 we established our first satellite office at CityLink Center. The center is located in Cincinnati's West End neighborhood and provides services as a one-stop center to assist people in getting out of poverty. Cincinnati Works supplies the work component. We are fully staffed there and can also draw on other services provided at CityLink.

This partnership has been very productive. Last year we assisted people in obtaining 200 employments with a 71% retention rate after one year. There are also 37 CityLink members in advancement, and 43 have obtained self-sufficiency (our goal for every job seeker). We recently opened another satellite office in the Madisonville Education and Assistance Center (MEAC), a nonprofit organization founded in 1986. They focus on poverty alleviation, including emergency relief and literacy. This partnership will leverage MEAC's services to help members meet basic needs and improve literacy while benefiting from Cincinnati Works' employment and financial coaching. Together we will be able to assist individuals navigating out of poverty and onto the path of self-sufficiency.

Another satellite office is being established in Roselawn. Our partner there is the Summit Community Center, located on the campus of the New Prospect Baptist Church. In addition to offering services for adults like our other satellites, we will be piloting another program designed to prepare at-risk, low-income 16–18-year-olds to become successful, educated, working adults. The Navigator program is a yearlong curriculum broken into four phases: Pre-Employment Skills, Financial Literacy, Communication Skills, and Professionalism and Networking. A community in South Carolina is already using this program.

Poverty in the Greater Cincinnati area has been increasing at a shocking rate. Cincinnati now has the seventh-highest rate of people living in poverty in our nation and ranked second-highest in child poverty out of 76 major U.S. cities in 2012. We may need more than five satellites to help get this unacceptable condition under control. Fortunately our city leaders have recently come together and agreed that poverty is a major problem in Cincinnati, and they are in the process of setting measurable goals to start reducing it.

Afterword

*"They are not dead who live in lives they
leave behind. In those whom they have
blessed they live a life again."*

–Hugh Robert Orr

Early in September 2008, at the invitation of nationally
recognized experts on poverty Ruby Payne and Philip
DeVol, Dave spoke about the magic of the workforce model
we've developed to a gathering of 60 people representing
19 different organizations, all of which were interested in
trying to end poverty in their communities. He talked about
the everyday miracles we've seen in the lives of thousands of
people. With the passion and absolute conviction of a zealot,
he told his listeners that he knew that it was possible to help
the poor become self-sufficient and that our model offered
hope to people whom most had written off as being beyond
hope. "Our model has consistently shown that through careful
research and thoughtful response, we can help end the cycle
of poverty," he concluded.

The next day he flew out to begin his second annual month-
long hike on the Appalachian Trail. To celebrate turning 70,
he'd decided to take a month off every year to hike the trail
in segments until he completes it. He uses that solitary time
in the mountains to contemplate what God wants from him
and what our next steps should be. On this second trek he said

he reached a point where he surrendered. "I realized that this journey has always been out of my hands," he told me when he returned. "It's about where God wants to take it."

When Dave returned to the office we share at Cincinnati Works, Glenna showed him a stack of messages. He'd gotten calls from around the country wanting to know about our model. Many people have visited Cincinnati Works to observe our processes, and Dave has made numerous presentations in other cities. He has committed himself to helping other communities get their own pilot programs off the ground. To date he has assisted more than 20 communities in using the Cincinnati Works model, and they are putting people to work. We don't know where all this will go, but we are delighted that impoverished people in other cities are becoming self-sufficient through a program that duplicates our process.

A generous three-year strategic partnership grant from the Carol Ann and Ralph V. Haile Jr./U.S. Bank Foundation enabled Cincinnati Works to move into a much-needed new space after a decade in the old one. The numbers of people we were helping continued to grow, and we simply ran out of room. Our new office offers an open floor plan, which is fitting since we believe the sky is the limit in terms of how many people we can help. Soon, though, we may need even more space!

Peggy Zink joined Cincinnati Works as president in 2009. She is a multitasker, totally committed to the mission, pays close attention to the numbers, and is well respected by our community.

Dave and I continue to share an office because we enjoy this adventure and love experiencing it together. Dave concentrates on helping other communities build initiatives based on the Cincinnati Works model—and on hiking the Appalachian

Trail, which he hopes he will finish next year. I find things to do in the office because I really enjoy meeting our members. The highlight of my day is introducing myself and receiving a wide grin, a handshake, and a profuse thank you for starting Cincinnati Works. We won't be around forever, but we believe that because of the need for programs that reduce poverty and because of the many committed people who are and will be involved with Cincinnati Works and the offshoots of our model, this grand vision will live on without us. This thought is very humbling to Dave and me.

My fond hope in writing this book is to bring a clearer understanding about people living in poverty and to present the many issues involved when working with them. I have also attempted to dispel some of the myths that exist about this population. I've shared many examples of ways we have tried to assist our members. My hope is that I have been transparent about what worked and what didn't, as well as about the issues that we are still trying to solve.

I passionately hope that this book will stimulate community support for community goals, a holistic approach to families, collaboration, and outcome-based programs so that we can reduce poverty in a significant way each year for this generation and the generations to come. Then more of our citizens will be able to give back to our communities and have a chance to share in the American Dream. What we do every day makes a lasting impact on society. We are creatively, holistically, and economically making the world a better place—one member, one job at a time.

–Liane Phillips
August 2016

APPENDIX

Staff Positions

Our program mobilizes a team of professionals who systematically provide a full array of services for each job seeker as he or she not only finds a job, but stays on it, succeeds, and advances. The team that serves our members includes the following:

Customer service representative (CSR): A CSR is usually the first staffer to interact with applicants and a crucial person to make them feel welcome and to answer questions.

Recruiter: The recruiter builds the partnerships with community organizations to recruit participants. When job seekers arrive, the recruiter gives the briefing on what Cincinnati Works offers its members, explains the services and opportunities, then does a short one-on-one interview to steer people through the application process.

Community engagement specialist: The community engagement specialist markets Cincinnati Works services to prospective applicants to increase member enrollment at all Cincinnati Works locations. Ongoing, permanent relationships with other organizations ensure these organizations use Cincinnati Works as a tool in their economic and residential development goals.

Workshop facilitator: The workshop facilitator coordinates and conducts the job readiness and retention program and communicates appropriate and inappropriate job behavior to job seekers in a classroom setting.

✓ **Professional development coach/staffing specialist (job coach):** The job coach establishes and maintains direct service activities for Cincinnati Works members by supporting job retention and case management. Additional responsibilities may include job acquisition services facilitated through the Cincinnati Works core employer relationships, as well as self-directed job development. The job coach creates and facilitates an individual job search action plan with each member to increase job search activity and promote soft skills growth in areas like employer communication, business professionalism, mock interviews, etc. The job coach also communicates open job leads to aid members in finding employment.

✓ **Advancement coach:** The advancement coach manages program services that support members in advancement with employment, as well as development and completion of career strategies that enable self-sufficiency. The advancement coach also updates, implements, and evaluates self-sufficiency and professional development classes and processes and recommends program improvements.

Financial coach: The financial coach provides direct services to low- to moderate-income members of Cincinnati Works who are enrolled as Financial Opportunity Center participants. The financial coach is responsible for assisting members in developing plans of action that are intended to help them reach their goals and achieve financial stability. The financial coach is expected to focus services in a one-on-one counseling format. However, the coach might also conduct classes and workshops on topics such as budgeting, credit building, and banking products. The financial coach will work with the job coach to ensure the member is getting assistance across these three major service areas.

Chaplain: The chaplain addresses the spiritual needs of members, restoring hope and encouraging responsibility, stability, and resilience.

Legal coordinator: The legal coordinator assists with expunging criminal records and dealing with landlord/tenant issues, bankruptcy, child support, and other legal issues.

Employer relations specialist: The employer relations specialist interacts with employers to keep job openings coming, then checks in with supervisors to see how the new hires are working out.

Director of clinical services: The director of clinical services provides counseling and refers needs for more serious intervention to appropriate venues.

Phoenix outreach coordinator/mentor: In a collaborative effort, the Phoenix outreach coordinator/mentor establishes and maintains relationships within the community to promote awareness of the Cincinnati Works Phoenix program and alternatives to gang life. The Phoenix outreach mentor provides support groups and additional services to Cincinnati Works Phoenix members who are gang involved or at risk of becoming involved. The mentor works as a liaison both internally and externally to support, mentor, and coach members, as well as link members to a wide range of programs.

Navigator coordinator: The navigator coordinator is responsible for managing the program startup efforts, recruiting participants, and directing all navigator service delivery. The coordinator helps establish and maintain relationships with the partner network and the local neighborhood to facilitate strong community ties, build recruiting channels, and ensure comprehensive support of program participants and their mentors.

INDEX

ABOUT THE AUTHORS

Liane Phillips currently serves as interim president of Cincinnati Works, the organization which she co-founded. In 2001 *The Cincinnati Enquirer* named Liane Phillips one of its Women of the Year, and the College of Mount St. Joseph awarded her an honorary doctorate. In 2003 the Cincinnati Bengals presented her the Community Quarterback Award, and in 2005 she and her husband Dave won the Visiting Nurse Association's Caring Award.

Phillips served on the education panel for Cincinnatus, an organization that works to improve the city, and on committees and task forces for the Second Congressional District of Ohio Anti-Drug Coalition, the 1996 PRIDE World Drug Conference, the Center for Economic Education's Achieving Career Potential, and the unemployment subcommittee of the Cincinnati City Council Committee of Finance and Labor, where she was appointed to the job creation task force.

Phillips was also on the regional advisory council of Just Say No International and served as conference chairperson of Prevention Works! for the 1994 Business and School Partnership Conference. She has held a number of positions in the Greater Cincinnati Literacy Task Force and was named volunteer of the year for Pro-Kids (CASA). She also volunteered for the Inter-Agency Council on Child Abuse and Neglect and served on the board of directors and programs committee of Los Angeles Youth Programs, Inc. Liane has been active in United Way as part of the subcommittee for St. Joseph Orphanage and United Way's Self-Sufficient People Vision Council.

Her education includes graduate studies in counseling psychology from Pepperdine University, a master's degree in education from Xavier University, and a B.S. in education from the University of Cincinnati. Dave and Liane have been married for 50 years and have three sons: Scott, an attorney; Todd, a veterinarian; and Brett, a probation officer. They have nine grandchildren.

Echo Montgomery Garrett is a journalist with 25 years' experience and author of *My Orange Duffel Bag: A Journey to Radical Change; Dream No Little Dreams,* the authorized story of Clay Mathile and The Iams Company; *How To Make a Buck and Still Be a Decent Human Being: A Week with Rick Rose at Dataflex;* and ghost writer of *Tales From the Top: Ten Crucial Questions from the World's #1 Executive Coach.*

A former contributing writer to *Money, BusinessWeek, Management Review, Investor's Business Daily,* and *The Atlanta Business Chronicle,* Garrett has been published in more than 75 national magazines, newspapers, and websites, including *INC. Magazine, The New York Times, Chief Executive, The Atlanta Journal-Constitution,* and ABCNews.com. She has been interviewed on *Good Morning America,* CNBC, CNN, NY-1, and has done more than 50 radio interviews supporting book projects and magazine articles. As editor-in-chief of *Atlanta Woman* magazine, her first issue took the gold for best single issue out of 300 entrants at the 2005 GAMMA awards sponsored by the Magazine Association of the Southeast. A graduate of Auburn University with a degree in journalism, Echo is a member of the Authors Guild, the American Society of Journalists and Authors, Investigative Reporters and Editors, and the Atlanta Press Club.

Married to Kevin Garrett and mother to teenage sons Caleb and Connor, Garrett resides in Marietta, Georgia, and serves as a board member for Gift for a Child/The Heart Gallery Southeast, an organization that encourages adoption from the foster care system, and The Ruby Slipper Project, which grants interior design makeovers to families in need.

For more information or to contact Garrett, please visit www.EchoGarrett.com.

Liane Phillips' portion of the proceeds of this book will go to fund the effort to expand the model and to the continued efforts at Cincinnati Works. A portion of Echo Garrett's proceeds will also go to help expand the model.

To learn more about Cincinnati Works, please visit www.CincinnatiWorks.org.

"Speak up and judge fairly; defend the rights of the poor and needy."
—Proverbs 31:9